VOID

Library of
Davidson College

GOVERNMENTS & CORPORATIONS IN A SHRINKING WORLD

TRADE & INNOVATION POLICIES IN THE UNITED STATES, EUROPE & JAPAN

by Sylvia Ostry

A COUNCIL ON FOREIGN RELATIONS BOOK

GOVERNMENTS & CORPORATIONS IN A SHRINKING WORLD

GOVERNMENTS & CORPORATIONS IN A SHRINKING WORLD

TRADE & INNOVATION POLICIES IN
THE UNITED STATES, EUROPE & JAPAN

Sylvia Ostry

COUNCIL ON FOREIGN RELATIONS PRESS
NEW YORK • LONDON

COUNCIL ON FOREIGN RELATIONS BOOKS

The Council on Foreign Relations, Inc., is a nonprofit and nonpartisan organization devoted to promoting improved understanding of international affairs through the free exchange of ideas. The Council does not take any position on questions of foreign policy and has no affiliation with, and receives no funding from, the United States government.

From time to time, books and monographs written by members of the Council's research staff or visiting fellows, or commissioned by the Council, or written by an independent author with critical review contributed by a Council study or working group are published with the designation "Council on Foreign Relations Book." Any book or monograph bearing that designation is, in the judgement of the Committee on Studies of the Council's board of directors, a responsible treatment of a significant international topic worthy of presentation to the public. All statements of fact and expressions of opinion contained in Council books are, however, the sole responsibility of the author.

For more information about Council publications, please write the Council on Foreign Relations, 58 East 68th Street, New York, NY 10021, or call the Publications Office at (212) 734-0400.

Copyright © 1990 by the Council on Foreign Relations, Inc.
All rights reserved.
Printed in the United States of America.

This book may not be reproduced, in whole or in part, in any form (beyond that copying permitted by Sections 107 and 108 of the U.S. Copyright Law and excerpts by reviewers for the public press), without written permission from the publishers. For information, write Publications Office, Council on Foreign Relations, 58 East 68th Street, New York, NY 10021.

Library of Congress Cataloguing-in-Publication Data

Governments and corporations in a shrinking world / trade and innovation policies in the United States, Europe, and Japan / by Sylvia Ostry.
    p.   cm.
    Includes bibliographical references.
    ISBN 0-87609-079-X
    1. Commercial policy.   2. International trade.   3. Technological innovations—Government policy.   4. Competition, International.   5. International business enterprises. I. Title.
HF1411.O689   1990
362'.3–dc20   89-20978
                                                                               CIP

90 91 92 93 94 95 96 PB 10 9 8 7 6 5 4 3 2 1

*I would like to extend my
warmest thanks to*

Kenneth W. Dam

*without whom this project would not
have been completed*

CONTENTS

Foreword—*Kenneth W. Dam* ix
1. Introduction 1
2. Trade Policy 17
3. Innovation Policy 53
4. Conclusions 79

Appendix
    Council on Foreign Relations Study on
    The Search for Stability: Business and
    Government in an Interdependent World 111

Glossary of Abbreviations and Acronyms 115

Index 117

About the Author 123

FOREWORD

Kenneth W. Dam

The October 1987 stock market crash, which was felt across the globe; the role of the FAX machine, electronic mail networks, and satellite broadcasting in the June 1989 revolt in China; and the more recent events in Eastern Europe aptly demonstrate that we are living in a shrinking world. The information and telecommunications revolutions have blurred boundaries and have rendered borders almost obsolete. Now documents can be transmitted across oceans in a matter of seconds. But as the world shrinks and every country becomes more vulnerable to events beyond its borders, national governments are taking steps to establish advantages for their corporations over foreign competitors, especially in high-technology industries. Policies adopted in Washington, Brussels, and Tokyo are increasingly inconsistent with one another, and there is no international arbiter to resolve differences of opinion over which are fair and which are unfair.

In this book, Sylvia Ostry, the former Canadian ambassador for the Uruguay Round of multilateral trade negotiations and the prime minister's personal representative for the economic summit, surveys the emerging international economic order on trade and innovation policies, and focuses on the vast differences in the corporate-government interface in the political economy of policymaking within the Triad: the United States, the European Community, and Japan. She foresees increasing friction and conflict within the Triad. But she does more than just identify emerging problems; she makes recommendations for overcoming the resulting frictions.

Governments & Corporations in a Shrinking World grew out of a Council on Foreign Relations' study group—"The Search for

Stability: Business and Government in an Interdependent World"—that met six times between April and November 1989. I had the privilege of chairing this group, which consisted of corporate executives, policymakers, and academics (see the Appendix). Representatives from eighteen global corporations from the United States, Europe, and Japan had a voice around the study group table. Those corporate representatives were extremely helpful in responding to Sylvia's ideas and in provoking discussion; the study could not have been carried out without their assistance, or that of the policymakers and academics who participated as well.

Nonetheless, this study is Sylvia's and hers alone. Those who know her know that she does not pull punches. She is always candid and often provocative. She deserves great credit for designing the study, executing it, and producing a highly readable book in a timely fashion.

Sylvia undertook the research for this book and wrote it while she was the first Volvo distinguished visiting fellow at the Council on Foreign Relations. On behalf of the Council, I would like to thank the Volvo North American Corporation for its generous funding both for her research and for her support. She was also assisted by her new colleagues at the University of Toronto where she has now become chairman of the Advisory Board and senior research fellow at the Center for International Studies. Her support at the University of Toronto was funded by a grant from the Donner Canadian Foundation and the Ontario Ministry of Treasury and Economics.

On behalf of Sylvia, I would like to thank those members of the study group who went above and beyond the call of duty by commenting extensively on this manuscript when it was in draft form. At the risk of forgetting someone, I should mention C. Michael Aho, Jagdish Bhagwati, Travis Brooks, Bill Diebold, Gary Horlick, Peter Kenen, Charles Levy, Peter Ludlow, Kazuo Nukazawa, Joan Spero, Masao Uchibayashi, Raymond Vernon, Alan Wolff, and John Zysman.

The study group was ably coordinated by C. Michael Aho, director of economic studies and the International Trade Project at the Council, with the assistance of Alison von Klemperer and

Dorothy Price. Dorothy also served admirably as the group's rapporteur. Other members of the Council staff contributed valuably to the project. Thanks are particularly due to Suzanne Hooper and David Kellogg of the publications department. Finally, as chairman of the study group, I would like to thank personally Peter Peterson, chairman of the board of the Council, Peter Tarnoff, president, and Nicholas Rizopoulos, vice president for studies, for their unwavering support throughout the duration of the project.

This is a study. But it has a bottom line. After you have finished reading it, I believe you will agree that each of us in business, government, and private life has a great deal to do to minimize economic frictions among countries, as advances in information and telecommunications technologies draw us ever closer together.

Kenneth W. Dam is Vice President, Law and External Relations, at IBM.

1

INTRODUCTION

The multilateral institutions—the International Monetary Fund (IMF), the World Bank, and the General Agreement on Tariffs and Trade (GATT)—were established after the Second World War in a world far less interdependent than today's. The trade, financial, and technology links that now draw countries more closely together have dramatically changed the policy context for governments, international institutions, and multinational corporations. The GATT, for many reasons, has found it increasingly difficult to adapt to these changes. The multilateral trading system is clearly under stress. One alternative, a trend to bilateral or regional blocs and to more unilateral behavior by powerful trading countries, is likely to accelerate should the Uruguay Round of the GATT fail to deliver an acceptable package. Such a package would have to include the extension of GATT rules well beyond traditional border measures into the domain of what are essentially domestic policies. Yet even as this ambitious eighth round of GATT negotiations draws to a close, new sources of international friction, which lie outside its agenda, are on the horizon.

One major change in the present environment is the growing role of the "global"[1] corporations, the multinationals that increasingly operate on the basis of a worldwide rather than a multicountry strategy. The international economic environment of the coming decades will be shaped not by governments or international institutions but by the *interaction* of the two main actors, governments and global corporations—especially in the Triad: the United States, Europe, and Japan.

Indeed, the present phase of accelerating world integration is dominated less by increasing trade linkages than by rapidly growing investment and technology flows facilitated by the exploding financial linkage of the 1980s. The chief agents of interdependence in this phase are the global enterprises. Neither governments nor these corporations have a comprehensive overview of the complex web of interaction, including the indirect consequences of a given policy—which often outweigh its short-run, direct impact—and the way that the policy process in one region is affected by, and in turn influences, that in other regions. Yet it is precisely this concatenation, drawn ever tighter by global interdependence, that will determine the international flows of trade, investment, and technology.

Hence it is the interaction between governments and global corporations that will determine the future of multilateralism. Nonetheless, little research has focused on this interaction, or what is termed the political economy of policymaking in the Triad.

To be more precise, such studies of the political economy of policymaking as exist are by and large concentrated on U.S. trade policy. Much less is available on Japan or the European Community (EC), and almost no international comparative analyses or examination of the interrelationship among the policy processes in each region appear in the literature.

To tackle this subject in a comprehensive fashion would clearly involve detailed and careful case studies.[2] The present study bears no pretense of comprehensiveness. First, it is confined to global corporations and thus does not purport to examine the multifaceted business-government relationships that would include national firms or other groups that deal with governments in the policy process, such as trade unions or farmers. Discussions in the Council on Foreign Relations' working group, which included representatives of American, Japanese, and European global corporations as well as policy and academic experts (see Appendix), were helpful in providing information about the international policy process. But clearly, if this analysis provides insights, their chief merit may well be to point the way to further, more intensive research agendas.

A basic assumption that propelled the Council project was the idea that global corporations should be "natural stakeholders" in a rules-based multilateral system. This was assumed for one fundamental, indeed elementary, reason—their need for stability and predictability. Indeed, it may be argued that the only genuine public good aspect of an international trade regime—the GATT—is stability itself, or the reduction of uncertainty. The use of rules to reduce uncertainty and thereby increase private investment by fostering a long view, essential to efficient resource allocation, was central to Keynes's proposals on international monetary reform,[3] but it is just as relevant to the trading regime.

Nonetheless, the behavior of the global corporations in the present policy context reveals no such consistent attachment to the GATT-based system of rules. Only in the U.S. case could one say—with increasing tentativeness, by the way—that the idea of natural stakeholders has any credibility. So the basic assumption proved quite erroneous if judged either by corporate behavior—revealed preference—or by opinion and attitude. The reasons why the assumption proved wrong are not and could not be fully explicated in this study, although one factor that does seem relevant to the differences is cultural, historical, and institutional influences. Seen in this context, the policy activism of American corporations reflects the unique American system of governance. The basic indifference of the European and Japanese enterprises is similarly a historic, institutional, and cultural phenomenon; therefore, if it changes, it will do so slowly and with difficulty in response to international pressure.

Other likely reasons obtain as well. Even in the case of the activist U.S. multinationals, the slowness of GATT procedures and what is regarded as the excessively cumbersome nature of negotiations among over 90 countries are causing growing frustration. In the past negotiations were simpler (mainly over tariffs), and fewer countries were involved. The contrast between the rapidity of change in the world economy and the slow and painful response of the trading institution is very striking to many businessmen. (A good example is in the key area of intellectual property. The United States proposed a counterfeiting code in 1978. Measures to deal with counterfeiting, after more than a decade of mounting loss to corporations in industrialized countries, may be adopted in 1990 as part of the Uruguay Round.) The corporations too often contrast this phenomenon of slowness in the GATT with the greater ease and efficiency in dealing with their own or even their host governments. A latent preference for regionalism or bilateralism is thus emerging for what appear to be simple, practical reasons.

Most of all, perhaps, because the GATT has lacked a continuing and structured relationship with business—in contrast, for example, to the Business and Industry Advisory Committee of the Organization for Economic Cooperation and Development (OECD), or to the close ties between financial enterprises and the IMF or World Bank—it seems remote and unrelated to any immediate concerns of the global enterprises. There is little identification of the mutual interests between them.

Finally, a more fundamental phenomenon may be at work. Few firms are truly global, but many are globalizing through a new wave of investment and corporate alliances. Perhaps truly global firms, having the options of trade or investment, will become neutral or indifferent both to exchange rate changes and to trade rules, in the belief that they can adapt, albeit at some cost, to any "rules" governments establish. We shall return to this issue in the final chapter; the important point here is that the costs of adaptation to a distorted but stable system are far less than those imposed by uncertainty and unpredictability. In a stable system risk can be reasonably assessed; uncertainty makes risk assessment extremely difficult.

This issue of uncertainty is central to the focus of the research, for it is clear that a number of incipient trends on the horizon of the international economic scene are creating pervasive and increasing uncertainty about the future evolution of the world trading system. At the same time, as the decade of the 1990s begins, the industrialized economies are enjoying an unprecedented long period of growth, and trade and investment are buoyant. The steady increase, since the mid-1970s, of the so-called new protectionism (border and domestic nontariff measures for mature industries) may have affected the direction of trade flows, but clearly has been porous enough to permit a healthy pickup in total trade as the rate of growth in investment and output has increased.[4] As I will argue in this and subsequent chapters, another powerful source of international friction or protectionist pressure on both the trade and the investment fronts is now emanating not from the traditional import-defensive industries but from technologically sophisticated manufacturing industries, whose products form an increasing share of trade among industrialized countries. Thus the apparent paradox—increasing trade and increasing protectionism—should not be considered immutable. To base international policy on such an assumption would be to make policy in a rearview mirror.

The Uruguay Round of GATT negotiations will, if successful, significantly extend and strengthen the rules-based multilateral trading system. It is the most comprehensive and ambitious in the history of the GATT and, more than any previous round, is focused on the international spillover of domestic policies. Launched at Punta del Este, Uruguay, in September 1986, it is to be concluded by December 1990. The fifteen negotiating groups cover four principal categories:

- *Market access,* including tariff and nontariff barriers in manufactured goods and, for the first time in 40 years, in agriculture.

- *So-called new issues* of trade-related investment measures (such trade-related aspects of intellectual property rights as patents and copyrights) and trade in services.

- *Reform of GATT rules,* such as rules concerning subsidies and the actions governments may take to offset them (countervailing duties), rules about measures governments may take when import surges threaten serious injury to domestic industries (safeguards), rules addressing government actions to counter dumping, and rules concerning government procurement.

- *Measures to strengthen GATT as an institution* by establishing more effective and streamlined dispute settlement procedures, creating better links between the GATT and the World Bank and the IMF, instituting procedures to review countries' trade policies and actions, and giving more ministerial direction to the GATT's work.

But, as we will see in detail, the particular combination of domestic and international policy that is geared to high-technology industries—innovation policy—and the new wave of internationalizing investment lie well outside the mandate of even a greatly strengthened GATT at the present. Indeed, the Uruguay Round should be seen as the beginning and not the end of the reform required to adapt the postwar system established by the United States at a time of undisputed political and economic dominance. However, as will be emphasized in what follows, the transition to the multipolar world of the Triad may confront not simply a deficit in multilateralism but a vacuum at the center: an odd trio of a leader without hegemony and two potential hegemonies reluctant to assume leadership in multilateral institutional reform. And, as will be seen, many corporate players that are global in corporate planning are still regional or national in policy outlook.

The remainder of this chapter is devoted to sketching out the main background factors or incipient trends now discernible that are creating the environment of uncertainty about the evolution of the world trading and economic system.

MACRO BACKGROUND FACTORS

Since the early 1980s the world trading system has been affected as much by macroeconomic, or financial, forces and policies as by the micro factors that are its traditional domain. As is well known, a powerful force fueling protectionist pressures in the United States in the first half of the decade was the wide swing in exchange rates and the rapid deterioration in the U.S. trade balance, with its attendant rise in unemployment. The fact that this condition stemmed from incompatible macro policy positions among the key industrialized countries of the Group of Seven (G-7)—the United States, Japan, Germany, France, the United Kingdom, Italy, and Canada—did not mitigate the impact on the American workers and businesses that suffered the consequences and demanded political redress.

As we shall see in the next chapter, while the full fury of the protectionist pressures has abated (in part because of the exchange rate realignment the G-7 initiated in 1985), and the Omnibus Trade Act of 1988 has been a vast improvement over most of its 300-plus ancestors of the earlier part of the decade, U.S. trade policy is now set on a new course, whose precise direction is not yet clear. Over the next few years, once again, a key element in how U.S. trade policy actually evolves is likely to be the current account positions of the United States and its main trading partners.

Several reasons lead to this assessment. The first relates to the fiscal deficit. Throughout the policy debate of the 1980s policymakers in the G-7 and economists reached near-universal agreement that a necessary (even, for some, sufficient) "solution" to the problem of the current account imbalances was a sustained and significant reduction in the U.S. fiscal deficit. That consensus view is beginning to erode both internationally and in the United States.

On the *international* front, while standard communiqué rhetoric still scolds the United States for lack of decisive action on the fiscal front, the heat has dissipated: the fiscal-solution-to-the-world's-problems tone has evaporated. The reason is quite clear in the June 1989 OECD *Outlook*: "assessing the likely sustainability of a given pattern of current balances has become increasingly difficult."[5] The threat of a dollar crisis—the best international argument to spur U.S. budget action—has become embarrassingly less credible in the face of reasonable exchange rate stability or, indeed, dollar strengthening (which, if continued, would seriously undermine U.S. competitiveness once again). As the OECD said: "in the more open international financial environment of the past decade, current account imbalances have proved financeable on a larger scale, and for longer, than would have been expected earlier."[6] The Bank for International Settlements was more straightforward, noting that "adjustment efforts have ceased to figure high on the policy agenda" and rightly emphasizing that "if the matter is to receive more attention, the limits of sustainability will have to be more clearly in view."[7] In the present context—that is, trade policy—the issue is not *financial* but *political* sustainability of the external deficit.

On the *domestic* front in the United States, the fiscal-deficit-doesn't-matter school has attracted more and more adherents and is certainly gaining strength in public opinion. As one analyst has observed, "the left of center finds common ground with the supply-siders of the far right" in arriving "at a common set of conclusions de-emphasizing the importance of the deficit."[8]

In effect, both international and domestic opinion seem to be converging on a newly emerging theme, that the U.S. budget deficit is largely a U.S. domestic problem, although it will continue to have a significant international impact. More important in terms of political dynamics, the "crisis" rhetoric is proving very difficult to maintain. The fiscal deficit "problem" is not immediate but will emerge only gradually over the long term (one author's "termites in the basement," or the *Economist*'s "prolonged wasting disease"[9]). Anorexia is unlikely to carry the same emotional charge as an imminent heart attack. As fiscal action diminishes in political weight, another consequence will be to raise the priority of micro policies, including trade and innovation policies (see below and chapter 3).

This consequence seems logical for several reasons. First, all forecasts by international agencies, while differing in detail, agree that the improvement in the U.S. current account imbalance has plateaued, at best. The bilateral balance with Japan, indeed, is forecast to widen in the future after recent diminution, and I shall return to this shortly. While U.S. fiscal action would certainly improve the outlook, that (as argued) seems increasingly unlikely (although eventually the "peace dividend" from disarmament may have an impact). Moreover, recent studies of the U.S. "twin deficits" stress the importance of other factors in explaining the evolution of the current account—factors such as U.S. household savings behavior (for which a budget surplus is the only practicable but increasingly elusive solution) but also structural "competitiveness problems," which are partly the result of the slowdown in capital formation during the high-deficit 1980s.[10] Be that as it may, these problems will require new micro policies, both domestic and international. The pressure for such policies is thus likely to build, both because they are considered essential in themselves and because, in the absence of fiscal action, the stalled current account adjustment process will once again create mounting popular demands in the United States to "do something" about the imbalances, especially in U.S.-Japanese trade.

In the early 1980s, one observer commenting on the growing pressure in the United States for "aggressive reciprocity" vis-à-vis Japan noted the widespread perception of "unequal access," stemming from other countries' "unfair" behavior. He remarked that "the real basis for the current perception of unequal access stems not from a careful analysis of protection itself, but primarily from growing frustration over the U.S. bilateral trade deficit with Japan, which reached $16 billion in 1981 and is expected to hit $20 billion to $22 billion in 1982."[11]

The result of that earlier frustration, after repeated unsuccessful "market opening" exercises at the sectoral level, was the 1988 Omnibus Act, and especially "super 301," which I will discuss in the next chapter. The bilateral trade deficit with Japan at present, however, is nearly three times the earlier figure.

In probing Japan's current account adjustment process, recent economic analysis raises puzzling questions about the role of the exchange rate. Under the impact of the high yen, Japanese industry undertook a number of structural measures that appear to have made Japanese exporters "currency-neutral." These measures included foreign direct investment in both the United States and the Asian newly industrializing economies (NIEs) and, more recently, in Europe. This permits the corporations to mitigate the impact of currency swings on profit by shifting output if necessary. In addition, a rapid and continuing move into higher-value-added products is making many Japanese exporters less price-sensitive.

Another element in the renewed concern about the U.S. bilateral balance with Japan has been concentrated on the atypically low Japanese import propensity, and a number of econometric studies have sought to estimate its extent and nature. In addition, recent studies have suggested that a marked differential exists between productivity growth in export-oriented sectors and in domestic sectors of Japanese industry, so that the real exchange rate (measured on the basis of *overall* prices or unit labor costs) significantly understates Japanese competitiveness.[12] This opens up the politically unappealing prospect, in the absence of other policy measures in both the United States and Japan, of further substantial and continuing U.S. dollar depreciation.

More generally, it is far from clear that American industry will be able to remain globally competitive without further dollar depreciation to offset prospective differentials between the growth rates of U.S. and foreign productivity:

> During the past decade, Japanese manufacturing productivity has been expanding at a 5.8% annual rate compared to 3.3% for the U.S. and 2.6% for Europe. Because of the dollar's decline during the late 1980's, American unit labour costs have risen by only 2.2% per annum compared to 5.0% for Japan and 3.2% for Germany (when their currencies are converted into dollars). But the price benefits of the 1985–1987 devaluation will soon fade if Japanese productivity continues to grow twice as rapidly as America's and the dollar remains constant in real terms. Since Japanese capital spending now exceeds America's in absolute terms and is twice as high on a per capita basis, it is probable that Japanese manufacturing productivity will remain in the 5–6% range during the early 1990's and that America's will not exceed 3.0%.[13]

On present indications of both U.S. fiscal policy and G-7 exchange rate policy aimed (broadly speaking) at stability, all these separate strands of analysis and argument presage greater political pressure for micro—that is, trade and innovation—policies to "deal with" the Japanese bilateral surplus.

Finally, the macro background picture with respect to the EC stands in sharp contrast to that of Japan. The persistent and growing current account surplus of Germany is increasingly oriented within Europe, while the bilateral balance with the United States is declining. Less and less inclination to analyze the German surplus within the context of the international adjustment process is evident in international forums. It is viewed, rather, as entirely a European issue to be dealt with (if any policy measures are required) as part of the ongoing process toward European Monetary Union. Furthermore, even the transatlantic debate over German fiscal policy (a possible quid pro quo of easing for U.S. tightening) has become muted in the face of the new growth buoyancy in Europe, attributed in part to the quickening momentum of Europe 1992. In sum, no large clouds on the U.S.–EC *macro* horizon are apparent that would stimulate trade-related friction for the foreseeable future. The focus will remain Japan.

MICRO BACKGROUND FACTORS: COMPETITIVENESS

The heightened profile of competitiveness as a major political and policy issue in the United States is double-stranded. One aspect, as just noted, is linked to the current account deficit and heavily centered on the U.S.–Japanese bilateral trade deficit. The other, also focused on Japan, is the idea of targeting "strategic" industries. (The word *strategic* is often used loosely, but the general meaning in the context of the competitiveness debate is leading-edge industries for which a domestic base is considered essential for economic or security reasons. See chapter 3.) At the level of popular opinion, but also partly supported by industrial policy advocates and some trade economists, is the growing conviction that Japan has successfully pursued such targeting policies (with the NIEs not far behind).

As we shall discuss in chapter 3, no consensus exists on the definition of targeting or of strategic industries, or, within the economics discipline, on policy prescriptions. Nonetheless, as I will also argue, the likelihood is far higher that new micro policy developments in the United States, in both trade and domestic policy, will be directed to "competitiveness" rather than (or in addition to) traditional import-blocking or other defensive industrial policies that are seen as anticompetitive in their effects and that run counter to the prevailing policy thrust of enhancing market forces (the OECD structural adjustment program).

Moreover, in this instance, the EC also enters the picture. Impelled by the Japanese paradigm, and reinforced by the implementation of Europe 1992, the EC has started to put in place elements of a policy strategy focused on competitiveness. Part of the strategy, perhaps unplanned, appears to be an increasingly active and "innovative" use of antidumping regulation.

More generally, throughout the OECD, governments are increasingly concerned with what is now being termed "innovation policy," seeking to integrate and update their industrial and science policies of the 1970s. The international implications of all these developments are by no means clear, but there are already, as will be seen below, grounds for concern about the potential to generate serious international friction.

REGIONAL TRADING BLOCS

The final background factor of note in the current climate is the growing interest in regional trading blocs.[14] The two developments that have triggered the current discussion are the recently concluded U.S.–Canada Free Trade Agreement (FTA) and the EC move to dismantle impediments to the free flow of goods, services, capital, and labor among member-states by the end of 1992, "Europe 1992."

The FTA and Europe 1992 are very different in both genesis and nature. Indeed, their coincidence in timing is accidental, not planned. Yet in the world trading system, both are highly significant developments that will foster integration in the two largest and richest markets of the world. So it is probably not surprising that despite their marked differences, these two regional developments have provoked questions about a possible new trend in the world trading system.

The origins of the FTA were quite dissimilar in the United States and Canada. In the United States, the bilateral policy was spawned by a need to quell the rising tide of protectionist pressure and the administration's growing frustration with the difficulties of launching a new round of multilateral negotiations, a pursuit it had followed without success since the early 1980s. The bilateral approach developed as a "strategic threat" policy to unblock the launch and to underline the significance of the "new issues": services, investment, and intellectual property. It was intended to warn the foot-draggers—especially the EC, fearful of the inclusion of agriculture as a central item on the multilateral agenda, and those opposing the new issues (some developing countries, led by Brazil and India)—that the GATT has feasible and attractive alternatives. (It is more than a little ironic that in the GATT today, the strongest critics of U.S. unilateralist or bilateralist tendencies are the countries that managed to delay the launch of the Uruguay Round for half a decade.)

For Canada, the overwhelming proximate reason for the bilateral initiative was fear of mounting U.S. protectionism (especially via the trade remedy laws), although equally important over the longer run was the objective of improved competitiveness to be gained from secure access to a market ten times the size of Canada's own.

While numerous factors, both political and economic, were at play in launching the move to full integration of the internal market in Europe (and the role of the European business community was of paramount importance as a catalyst), the external trading environment does not appear to have been a major consideration; in this respect the European initiative stands in sharp contrast to the genesis of the FTA. Moreover, almost no information was provided on the external implications of the internal measures until late 1988, three years after the introduction of the Single European Act, and even then a number of vital questions of concern to Europe's trading partners remained unanswered.

It was largely this lack of information that created uncertainty and suspicion in some quarters and evoked the talk of Fortress Europe. However unjustified such a term may prove to be, the combination of euphoria and vagueness that marked the European public discussion was bound to create disquiet abroad. This seems to have abated for the most part, and concern has now centered on specific issues, such as standards, rules of origin, and the precise meaning of reciprocity in new areas.

These coincident but unrelated policy actions in Europe and North America have, in turn, coincided with another regional development. In the Pacific area, not only have exports and imports surged in recent years, but major structural changes, catalyzed by the appreciation of the yen and the expansion of real domestic demand in Japan, are spurring regional integration via enhanced trade and investment linkages. For economic reasons, but also largely as a defensive response to the FTA and Europe 1992, a number of proposals for bilateral or regional arrangements (the former with the United States) in the Pacific area are now being proposed and analyzed. Clearly the political difficulties of institutional integration are immeasurably greater in the Pacific than in Europe, so much so that many observers discount its possibility. (It is too early to judge the outcome of the Australian initiative, introduced at the November 1989 Asia-Pacific Economic Co-Operation ministerial meeting, to work toward a Pacific OECD.) But the continuing interest in and exploration of bilateral and regional options in the Pacific region, combined with the European and North American developments, is generating a view in many quarters that regional blocs are an inevitability and only the question of timing remains unsettled.

Should the Uruguay Round fail, not only would the trend to bilateral and regional blocs accelerate, but without a strong multilateral institution at the center of the trading system, the discipline over the external policy of such blocs would be greatly weakened.

CONCLUSIONS

To summarize, a number of background factors in the current environment have the potential for generating significant changes in the evolution of the world trading system. Among the key unknowns are the future implementation of the U.S. 1988 Omnibus Trade Act and the trend to bilateral and regional bloc arrangements. In both cases, the outcome of the Uruguay Round will strongly influence developments.

In the United States, stalling of the global adjustment process is likely to focus increasing attention on micro policies, especially those directed to high-technology sectors. In the EC the launch of Europe 1992 was driven in large part by the premise that integration—a wholesale restructuring and rationalization of European industry—was the key to achieving improved competitiveness vis-à-vis the United States and Japan. To this, as we will see in subsequent chapters, has been added a panoply of "MITI-like" (the Ministry of International Trade and Industry in Japan) programs, especially in information technology and new developments in the use of antidumping. There has been no analysis of or, indeed, any reference to the international consequences of industrial targeting of strategic industries in the Triad.

Further, the European Commission's concern about the recent more frequent and novel use of antidumping in high-technology sectors seems to have induced an investment response by Japanese and Korean enterprises. More generally, the well-publicized growth estimates of a new Europe 1992, as well as uncertainty about several aspects of the external impact of EC internal regulations, may also be a factor governing investment decisions of third-country enterprises to locate in the Community. It seems probable that continuing discussion about the emergence of regional blocs will influence corporate behavior (a presence in each bloc), as well as government trade policy.

It must be noted, of course, that multinational enterprises rarely make investment decisions on the basis of only one consideration; rather, they have a variety of aims and causes. For example, one common objective in all corporate strategy is risk reduction. In the 1980s the fear of U.S. protectionism would have logically dictated a policy of greater foreign direct investment in North America. Moreover, today the increased research and development (R&D) costs required in the race for the technological frontier have undoubtedly stimulated a wave of corporate alliances as a basis for technology transfer or cost sharing. And so on.

Moreover, a move by one multinational will induce a similar move by another, since imitation is a risk-avoiding strategy.[15] We may be at the onset of a new wave of "follow the leader" internationalization, although most of the underlying pressures today are different from those in the 1970s.

Nor should we assume that because trade and investment flows were complementary in the 1960s and 1970s, such a relationship will hold for the future. New technology and changing corporate strategy—for example, flexible manufacturing—will provide a new set of incentives for deployment of productive resources closer to final markets. But governments' pressure to secure "quality" investment within their frontiers will also have to be factored into corporate decision-making. Negotiations between governments and corporations about the specifics of foreign direct investment and technology transfer may become as important in the industrialized countries tomorrow as they are in much of the developing world today. Yet no multilateral rules cover this development, although the Uruguay Round may begin to deal with some aspects via the negotiations on trade-related aspects.

The following chapters will explore these policy issues in greater detail by examining recent developments in policymaking in the trade and innovation fields. The focus will be on the international implications of these developments, and the final chapter will present some recommendations designed to grapple with these new pressures in the world trading system.

2

TRADE POLICY

It has often been said that no policy is as domestic as international trade policy. This was always the case, but it seems more glaringly obvious today, when tariffs are no longer the key issue in negotiations. The blurring of international and domestic policies will be a recurrent theme of this study. But in the context of this discussion on the political economy of trade policymaking, the best example of this blurring is the GATT's Uruguay Round agenda. The most important—and most contentious—issues are agriculture, services, intellectual property, and investment. In these areas the trade frictions stem from government regulatory policies that were designed to achieve a range of domestic objectives, both economic and noneconomic, with little concern for or recognition of international spillover. Such negotiations are difficult precisely because they touch the exposed nerve of sovereignty, and the entire historical, cultural, and institutional fabric of differing societies.

A key aspect of the political economy of trade policymaking in the Triad concerns the interface between government and the business sector. The process whereby business interacts with government in the formulation and implementation of trade policy differs markedly in the United States, the EC, and Japan. In large part these differences also reflect historical, cultural, and institutional settings. But the *process* of policymaking affects the *substance* of policy, and it is therefore useful to explore these differences and assess their impact.

For that purpose I have chosen two aspects of policymaking. One concerns "high" policy,[1] the policy for the Uruguay Round. In high policy, decisions are effected by government officials subject to political accountability. The other aspect examined is the "low," or "technical," track of antidumping law. In low policy, decisions are "determined" by rules, precedents, and administrative regulations.

HIGH POLICY: THE URUGUAY ROUND

The complex agenda of the Uruguay Round touches on issues of major concern to many groups in the economy. The process by which differing views and interests are factored into a government's strategy is thus a matter of considerable importance to the outcome of the negotiations. This is especially true in the case of the business community.

The U.S. System

A conventional model of the political economy of trade policy common to all democratic societies is characterized by a systemic domestic political bias against liberalization, since the benefits of protection are concentrated on relatively small, "special interests" and are felt almost immediately, while the benefits of liberalization are thinly diffused across the society and over time. The special interests thus tend to be well organized for seeking (and securing) protection (some of which is expressed by the trade remedy laws), whereas the proponents of liberalization have little incentive to organize and exert political pressure, but believe they will get a free ride on the liberalization that others, more directly in charge, will secure.

While this conventional view is basically true, in recent years, as a result of rapidly expanding international linkages, special interests *against* protection for specific products have become more active. These antiprotection interests are a diverse group: they represent industrial users of the product, retailers (if consumer products are involved), exporters who are concerned about retaliation, and, increasingly, foreign governments and subsidiaries of foreign multinationals.[2] This development has helped mitigate the growth in *product-specific* protection in the United States over the past decade or more.

But our main concern here is with high policy—the Uruguay Round—rather than protection for specific products, such as autos, footwear, textiles, steel, coffee, or sugar. While the balance between special interests for and against product-specific protections will certainly affect the high policy *outcome* in the bargaining over the whole "package," it is the broad-based business coalitions, of which there are a considerable number in the United States, that are more heavily engaged in the Uruguay Round *process*. For the product-specific special interests, active and continuing participation in such a process is usually not worth their while (until the final deal is proposed), because it is too difficult for them to predict the outcome in terms relevant to their bottom line. The business coalitions, in contrast, are too diverse in product orientation to play an active role in specific protection, but instead focus on developing a broadly shared high policy position.

U.S. trade policy reflects the U.S. system of governance: the extraordinary diffusion of power established by the Constitution, the absence of a permanent bureaucratic elite, the emphasis on transparency; the multiple avenues for public participation in policymaking. To outsiders this seems to be a system of governance based on a rejection of government. A remark of Lord Keynes during World War II expresses the view of a mandarin of the British Whitehall model of permanent public service: "But you don't *have* a government in the ordinary sense of the word."[3]

Paradoxically, the role of the private sector in U.S. trade policymaking may be connected to the "absence" of government. The private-sector role is essentially one of *pluralist activism*. There are many business organizations, and no one "voice" speaks for the private sector. Often former government officials are involved, and their involvement contributes to the activism. Indeed, pluralist activism is also a characteristic of a public sector once described as "loose-jointed and unfocused."[4] High policy is seen as a responsibility as much of the senior levels of the business community as of the government. This applies to a broader range of issues than trade policy, of course. In the case of the Uruguay Round, the Business Roundtable and the Emergency Committee for American Trade (ECAT), both at the chief executive officer (CEO) level, as well as the much larger Chamber of Commerce and the National Association of Manufacturers, all play an active role. In this chapter, for purposes of highlighting the differences within the Triad, the focus is on the Advisory Committee on Trade Policy and Negotiations (ACTPN), a group established by the government for multilateral negotiations (see below). But that does not imply, of course, that the other business coalitions—or, indeed, the enormous number of diverse business lobbies in the United States—are not equally or at times more important. A full-scale international comparative analysis would clearly have to deal with the diversity of the American system.

The Constitution gave Congress primary responsibility for regulating "commerce with foreign nations." In view of the systemic bias to protectionism in all democratic societies and, in the United States, the susceptibility of a decentralized, undisciplined Congress to special interest pressures (it has been remarked that if a congressman had cannibals in his district, he would promise them missionaries for breakfast), only by building in *counterweights* could the U.S. trade policymaking system generate the liberalizing bent displayed during the postwar period.

In one detailed analysis of American trade politics, the author observed that since the disaster of the Smoot-Hawley Act during the Great Depression, the American system for trade policymaking has constituted the "development of . . . anti-protectionist counterweights, devices for diverting and managing trade-restrictive pressures."[5] (The trade remedy laws, which will be discussed below, are an integral part of the counterweight system.)

The precise nature of these counterweights has changed over time, reflecting different arrangements whereby Congress sought to shift the pressure from special interests onto the executive while not entirely yielding constitutional power over policy or diminishing chances for reelection. The executive, traditionally internationalist and liberal, similarly required a delicate balance that would permit international negotiation without alienating domestic interests.

One key element in the counterweight system of U.S. trade politics is the private-sector advisory committee structure established under the 1974 Trade Act, which launched the Tokyo Round of GATT negotiations. This system is unique, the one area in which America engages in strategic planning to a greater extent than any of its trading partners. But this result was, at least in part, accidental:

> In 1975 Congress legislated the creation of an unprecedentedly major private sector advisory system for the Tokyo Round of Multilateral Trade Negotiations. The result was the establishment of forty-five committees and nearly 1000 advisers. Representatives of a wide variety of interests were constituted as a top level committee to give broad policy advice. Industry, agriculture and labor policy committees were also set up, supported by dozens of sectoral committees to provide technical advice. The trade negotiators, who drew all of their authority from Congress and would need to obtain Congressional approval of all but tariff agreements if any negotiating results were to be implemented, had to formulate objectives with the advisers and report to them any failures to follow their advice. The advisers would then report their views to Congress at the time the agreements were presented to Congress for approval.
>
> The political results were impressive. Congress, which had previously almost without exception rejected every trade agreement negotiated by the executive branch, gave a thumpingly lopsided endorsement to the Tokyo Round results—by a vote of 396 to 7 in the House, and 90 to 4 in the Senate. This was attributable not only to the political genius of U.S. Trade Representative Robert Strauss, but to the laborious process of private sector consultation, in which the adversary relationship between industry and government was forgotten, and trade officials and industry representatives worked closely together to promote U.S. commercial interests.[6]

This private-sector advisory process was reactivated for the Uruguay Round: indeed, it is a system that does not fully operate except during multilateral negotiations (and it was in force for the bilateral FTA). The 1988 Omnibus Act essentially reconfirmed the elaborate structure, shown in Figure 1. The committees are managed by the U.S. Trade Representative (USTR) in cooperation with the Departments of Commerce, Agriculture, Labor, and Defense.

The Advisory Committee for Trade Negotiations (ACTN)—renamed the Advisory Committee for Trade Policy and Negotiations in 1988—is the top oversight committee and has played an active role in shaping the overall agenda of the Uruguay Round. This is especially clear in the case of some of the new issues—services, trade-related intellectual property, and, most recently, trade-related investment measures. In cooperation with other U.S. business groups, it has launched international initiatives in these areas, with Americans taking the lead in

Advisory Committee for Trade Negotiations (ACTN)

Industry Policy Committee	Agriculture Policy Advisory Committee	Labor Advisory Committee for Trade Negotiations & Trade Policy	Defense Policy Advisory Committee	Services Policy Advisory Committee	Investment Policy Advisory Committee	International Steel Policy Advisory Committee	Commodity Policy Advisory Committee
Industry Sector Advisory Committee[1]	Agricultural Technical Advisory Committee[2]	Labor Sector Subcommittees[3]					
Industry Functional Advisory Committees[4]		Labor Functional Subcommittees[5]					
Industry Sector Advisory— Chairmen Committee		Labor Steering Subcommittee					

Notes:

1. Among the Industry Sector Advisory Committees are: aerospace equipment; capital goods; chemical and allied products; consumer goods; electronics and instrumentation; energy; ferrous ores and metals; footwear, leather, and leather products; industrial construction materials and supplies; lumber and wood products; nonferrous ores and metals; paper and paper products; services; small and minority business; textiles and apparels; transportation construction and agricultural equipment; wholesaling and retailing.
2. Agriculture Technical Advisory Committees include: cotton; dairy; fruits and vegetables; grain and feed; livestock and livestock products; oilseed and oilseed products; poultry and eggs; tobacco; sweeteners and tropical products.
3. The Labor Sector Subcommittees are: transportation equipment; lumber, wood, paper, stone, clay, and glass products; electronic equipment supplies and nonelectric machinery; services; food, agriculture products, chemical, plastic, and rubber products; textile apparel, leather products, and miscellaneous manufacturing industries.
4. The Industry Functional Advisory Committees are customs and standards.
5. The Labor Functional Subcommittees are government procurement, standards, and unfair trade practices.

Source: Executive Office of the President, United States Trade Representative, *A Preface to Trade* (Washington, D.C.: U.S. Government Printing Office, 1982), p. 86

FIG. 1. OFFICE OF THE UNITED STATES TRADE REPRESENTATIVE, ADVISORY COMMITTEE SYSTEM

securing the cooperation and support of European and Japanese corporations. In point of fact, in these instances, where careful and detailed analysis and proposals from the private sector were fed into the Geneva process, we have the only examples of meaningful and effective involvement by the business community in Europe and Japan, as an international private-sector "spillover" of U.S. business activism.

On the intellectual property issue, which is probably the agenda item of highest priority to key sectors of the U.S. business community, it is worth quoting at length from a speech by the chairman and CEO of Pfizer:

> In March of 1986, Ambassador Clayton Yeutter [USTR] called upon a group of us to work with our foreign counterparts to draw attention to the importance of intellectual property protection. Initially, I think Ambassador Yeutter hoped merely that business' efforts would assist the U.S. diplomatic position at the September 1986 ministerial meeting. What resulted was more lasting: a three-step process toward trans-national business cooperation. Something we really haven't had enough of. The *first* step had to do with U.S. companies. We were a loose alliance of diverse businesses—strange bedfellows. We needed to define our objectives and strategies more clearly—that between pharmaceuticals, movies or computers, for instance, we had to try to become a more cohesive unit. Our group, which included 13 major American corporations, became known as "The Intellectual Property Rights Committee," or IPC.
>
> The members of the group agreed among themselves on three areas critical to any international accord: certainly, first a code of minimum standards for copyrights, trademarks, patents, and appellation of origin issues. And then, naturally, an enforcement mechanism. And finally, dispute settlement. Without detailed and complete agreement on all three areas, international intellectual property protection accords would be meaningless.
>
> As a *second* step, the IPC moved to forge a consensus with the business communities in Europe and Japan. They were natural and important allies. And, it was hoped, a joint agreement involving the U.S., Europe, and Japan might exert a positive influence on the actions of the developing world—where, all too often, the theft of intellectual property is rampant.
>
> At first, the two major industrial "umbrella" organizations—UNICE [the Union of Industries of the European Community] in Europe, and Keidanren in Japan—were reluctant to join the IPC initiative. They feared that intellectual property was too new a subject to become part of the GATT, and they felt initially that intellectual property was, in any case, ill-suited to the Uruguay Round of trade discussions.
>
> Three IPC arguments—and a great deal of discussion—turned the tide of Japanese and European sentiment. First, it had become clear that WIPO [the World Intellectual Property Organization]—the worldwide body with the responsibility to defend in-

24 □ TRADE POLICY

tellectual property—was inadequate to the task. As part of the U.N. system, WIPO identifies with the special interests of the very governments in the developing world who abet the theft of intellectual property. This is not to say that WIPO does not continue to have an important role to play. It does, including—but not only—as the technical body concerned with intellectual property issues. Nevertheless, the GATT seemed the more appropriate means of administering the enforcement of international trading and investment norms.

Second, the massive scope of intellectual property theft was explained and documented by the IPC to our friends abroad, as was the threat to the future prosperity of developed economies should intellectual property theft continue to soar.

Finally, the IPC argued that—whereas WIPO and similar existing organizations lacked enforcement powers to combat this new form of trade distortion—much good could result if a combination of minimum standards, enforcement mechanisms, and dispute settlement could be instituted through the GATT. Intellectual property theft could be rendered easily recognizable. Violations could be made subject to direct consultations and mediation. And, by diminishing the need for unilateral retaliation, a GATT-based solution would do much to restore a sense of calm to trade relations.

IPC's thoughtfully-argued case eventually won the day. Given the speed with which intellectual property issues reached the world stage, and the brief two-year period over which the "Trilateral" discussions occurred, what resulted was truly remarkable.

In May 1988, UNICE, Keidanren, and the IPC met in Belgium to review intellectual property in the GATT. At the end of the session, an important three-way agreement emerged on all aspects of the subject. In the final report, the three business groups jointly stated their unequivocal support for including intellectual property protection in the Uruguay Round *and* set forth their proposals on minimum standards, enforcement mechanisms, and dispute settlement. This was the true multilateral approach that U.S. business had been hoping for.[7]

Thus the American business advisory system, designed as a counterweight to congressional susceptibility to protectionist pressure, has had largely unintended but, nonetheless, significant consequences for the world trading system. Of course, as already mentioned, the mandated structure is only one piece of a more elaborate system of business groups. But it is the chief conduit for government policy proposals into the Geneva negotiating process and an important conduit between the USTR and Congress. Many observers would argue that this system has, in fact, largely been a device for co-opting the business community.[8] Others would argue the opposite: that it has now become a device for policy capture (see below). Be that as it may, since government officials must provide a continuing account of the negotiations to these committees, it enhances the understanding by the private sector of the dynamics and constraints of the negotiations as a whole and, by creating some degree of personal identification with its success, changes behavior and expectations.[9] This is a very different situation from that in either the EC or Japan.

New Directions in U.S. Trade Policy

The pluralist activist political economy of U.S. high policy worked extremely well in the Tokyo Round and has had an important influence on the Uruguay Round agenda. Indeed, as noted, the activism has extended to taking a leadership role, for specific agenda items, that involved the corporations of other countries, both in the Triad and beyond. In the case of the ACTPN, the mandated coalition (and its predecessor of the Tokyo Round), the government had effectively established a conduit dedicated to multilateralism that was a near-unique example of U.S. strategic policy planning, albeit partly accidental. In contrast with Japan and the EC, to the outside observer it presents an impressive and unusual image of "U.S. Inc."

However, in such a structured system, the balance between policy co-option and policy capture is always delicate. A number of signs in the United States suggest that the traditional model of special interest protection, even as amended over the last decade by the emergence of special interest antiprotection in specific products, is changing. New directions are apparent both in the business community and in the government. At the very least the single focus of high policy on multilateralism and the GATT has gone. The United States now has a multitrack policy but with no very clearly defined set of objectives and policy instruments: *the new direction has an uncertain destination, but the journey has commenced.*

Several reasons account for the new direction. In the business community, as a number of experts have pointed out,[10] a "third force" has emerged since the late 1970s: global corporations in high-technology sectors that are not sympathetic to old-fashioned defensive import protectionism, but are not unequivocal antiprotectionists either. Their chief concern is to open foreign markets, especially in sectors where dynamic economies of scale or learning by doing is essential if rapidly growing R&D costs are to be sustained. As I will more fully discuss in the next chapter, this third force has been able to exploit effectively some "new directions" within the discipline of economics in making a plausible argument for a new market-opening approach targeted largely at Japan.

These changes in the business community coincided in the 1980s with a change in political climate and public perception best captured by the word "unfairness," a word with particularly strong resonance in the American psyche, as a forceful trope of the 1980s. The American sense of unfairness means many things: the belief that the American market is more open than any other in the world; that other governments intervene on behalf of their firms, whereas the U.S. government does not, or does so far less, and thus American industry faces "unfair" competition from governments; that the GATT has become inadequate in dealing with a range of domestic practices that "unfairly" distort trade and that, in the absence of multilateral rules, may be addressed only by unilateral definitions and actions; and that the United States has for decades carried an undue burden in supporting the liberal trading order.

The sense of unfairness is not an invention of the 1980s. The first overt and dramatic manifestation of policies stemming from this feeling was the Nixon-Connally actions in 1971, which marked the beginning of the end of the Bretton Woods system of fixed exchange rates. As one analyst remarks: "Not far below the surface [was] the feeling—tapped by Nixon and Connally—that the United States is carrying an unfairly large share of the burdens of maintaining security in the world and is somehow made a victim of the action of others in international trade."[11] The linking of trade and security is apt. Furthermore, the exceptional U.S. commitment to multilateralism was not due to an economist's proof of the virtues of free trade, but arose "out of the most elemental concerns: war and peace and the need for allies to be economically prosperous."[12] A liberal multilateral trading system was a means to an end in the achievement of these far broader "milieu goals."[13]

But a dramatic change in context occurred in the first half of the 1980s—marked by rising trade deficits; an overvalued dollar; regionally concentrated increases in unemployment; a weakened and weakening GATT, which made it more difficult for the American administration to persuade U.S. business that the multilateral system was an effective guardian of American interests; and growing concern about Japanese competitiveness in sector after sector. In response, the U.S. preoccupation with unfairness took out a new lease on life, creating powerful political pressures for a more aggressive trade policy and a consequent downgrading of the broader milieu goals that had guided U.S. administration policy over the postwar period.

In part to cope with the alarming rise in protectionist forces, the United States had been trying to launch a new round of GATT negotiations since the early 1980s, but the EC and some less-developed countries had successfully blocked these efforts. In January 1985, Ambassador William Brock, then USTR, asked the chairmen of the ACTN and the other official advisory committees to present their views on a new GATT round. Their report, issued in May 1985, contained a number of detailed recommendations not only from the official advisory committees but also from all the major private-sector business coalitions.

The chairmen's summary provided an interesting insight into the growing ambivalence of American business attitudes to multilateralism and the GATT since the triumphant end of the Tokyo Round. It reflected mounting frustration with the Reagan administration's trade and economic policies. After stressing that action was urgently required on the exchange rate and fiscal front, as well as on trade policy, the report stated:

> While support for a new round among the groups contacted ranged from strong support to strong opposition, the broadest consensus on a new round can best be described as moderate support provided that parallel efforts, both domestic and international, are undertaken to address the cause of America's trade problems. The broadest concern over entering a new round is that it would detract from, or even replace, efforts to develop a national trade policy.[14]

Elsewhere in the summary the chairmen describe that policy as a "tough U.S. trade policy."[15] As the report points out, support was strong *only among those groups advocating the inclusion of the new issues of services, intellectual property, and investment.* In sum, the American business view in mid-1985 (a year before the launch of the Uruguay Round) is best described as acceptance of multilateral negotiations on three conditions: a new exchange rate policy, elaboration of a "tough" U.S. trade policy, and inclusion of the new issues on the agenda of the multilateral trade negotiations (MTN).

The first two conditions were soon delivered. On September 22, 1985, the Plaza Accord launched the Reagan administration's new policy on the dollar. And, on September 23, President Reagan delivered a major, much-publicized speech on trade policy in which, in an effort to undercut the torrent of protectionist proposals flooding Congress, he recalibrated the American policy objective as *fair trade* ("Above all else, free trade is, by definition, fair trade") and announced his support, the first by an American president, for self-initiating the little-used section 301 of the 1974 Trade Act on unfair trade practices.[16]

On the same day, the USTR released the president's annual report on the Trade Agreements Program. In an appendix the report spelled out more fully a new U.S. national trade policy: a *multitrack policy* that included continuing efforts to launch a new GATT round; "the possibility of achieving further liberalization through the negotiation of bilateral free trade arrangements such as the one recently concluded with Israel"; and the third track of section 301:

> In the past, the United States has initiated Section 301 unfair trade investigations only in response to formal petitions for action from U.S. industries. The Administration will, as appropriate, also self-initiate such cases to address foreign unfair trade practices. . . . The Administration will take tactical measures aimed at eliminating unfair foreign trade practices and opening foreign markets if efforts to resolve such issues through consultations fail. The denial or limitation of access to the U.S. market may be a necessary measure in this process.[17]

From September 1985 to 1988, the United States used the threat of retaliation 26 times to extract trade concessions from ten trade partners on a bilateral and unrequited basis. The threat was sufficient in all but eight cases, when the administration actually used sanctions.[18] From the vantage point of many Americans, that is not a bad score!

The Omnibus Trade and Competitiveness Act of 1988 validated and more fully spelled out this third track in U.S. trade policy, especially in the so-called super 301 section. That part of the act called for identifying *countries* as unfair rather than just specific *practices* as the original 301 of the 1974 act provided. This new policy track has been given a number of different titles: aggressive reciprocity, aggressive bilateralism, and unilateralism, to name a few. Even the disagreement on titles is symptomatic of the uncertainty marking the policy thrust. This track centers on market opening and thus can be considered merely a tactical liberalizing adjunct to the Uruguay Round. It includes major elements of unilateralism (for example, in defining unfair practices and in determining their use) and is targeted bilaterally, the most important target at present being Japan. The "aggressive" label comes from the threat of retaliation as a means of achieving market opening. The new direction does not explicitly include, but provides a strong predisposition toward, results-oriented, as opposed to rules-oriented, policy. (This predisposition is best exemplified thus far in the U.S.–Japanese Semiconductor Agreement, described in the next chapter, which predates the Omnibus Act by two years.)

Many of the same elements of this new policy track are now appearing in proposals coming from important business groups. Early in 1989 the ACTPN report on U.S.–Japan trade suggested that the United States should identify sectors where its companies are competitive but are unable to gain access to the Japanese market, and negotiate "appropriate" import levels into Japan under threat of retaliation if necessary.[19] The ECAT has made a similar recommendation about Japan and has urged the Bush administration to "vigorously utilize the market access provisions of the 1988 Omnibus Trade Act, specifically section 301, as a further means of increasing access to the Japanese market for U.S. producers."[20] A 1989 report on U.S. manufacturing prepared for the Eastman Kodak Company is clearer than either the ACTPN or the ECAT in calling for a new multitrack policy: "U.S. trade policy needs urgent reconsideration. The GATT process has run out of steam and incremental benefits are small. The new emphasis should be an aggressive policy of market opening, in some instances by using the bilateral free trade approach."[21] The Kodak report, written by three well-known economists, is important in highlighting another emerging feature of the new direction in U.S. trade policy, the exploitation of the split among economists about policy prescriptions, a subject to which we will return below.

This rather lengthy digression on recent developments in the U.S. trade policy environment has been presented because of its implications for the world trading system as a whole. The political economy of U.S. trade policymaking is changing. Despite the continuing support for the Uruguay Round, neither the U.S. government nor the business community accepts any longer the preservation and strengthening of liberal multilateral trade as a *single, overriding objective.*

Moreover, if the Uruguay Round package proves to be unsatisfactory, this will trigger pursuit of both the bilateral free-trade track (for example, former U.S. Ambassador to Japan Mike Mansfield, former Senate Majority Leader Robert Byrd, and Senator Max Baucus have all promoted such an arrangement with Japan) and, to maintain the credibility of the Bush administration, more travel along route 301. Another way of putting this, perhaps, is that the milieu goals of high policy in the United States are visibly diminishing in priority. The significance of this can be fully appreciated only when viewed in the context of the political economy of policymaking in the other two blocs of the Triad.

The European Commission

The American system of pluralist activism has spawned a large descriptive and analytic literature on the political economy of trade policymaking in the United States. The U.S. system is highly transparent, both because that is the nature of American policymaking and because players in the trade system move in and out of government and the private sector, thus providing a source of valuable information and insight. In sharp contrast, the EC and Japanese systems are formidably opaque. Almost nothing in the way of published analytic studies exists. The brevity of the discussion in this chapter reflects that fundamental lack of information and analysis. Only detailed case studies of the EC and Japan—which would be far more difficult to do effectively than similar analyses for the United States—would help repair this serious lopsidedness.

As one commentator has observed, all international negotiations involve action on two fronts: external, between national representatives, and internal, among government bureaucracies, legislators, and interest groups.[22] The internal trade policy system of the United States, centered on active business input, was, as we have seen, designed to cope with, or "broker," interest group pressures acting on Congress, although its impact spread well beyond this original objective. In the EC the system was designed to broker the policy pressures emanating from member-states. Private groups have far less influence over the final outcome at the Commission level (except through the member-states), although on sensitive technical or bureaucratic issues the Commission negotiators work closely with representatives of Community-wide industrial groups on a *product-specific* rather than *generic* policy basis. Indeed, the Commission has encouraged the formation of these Community-wide sectoral groups to facilitate a Community rather than a national point of view.

The centerpiece of the EC system is the 113 Committee of national representatives (named after the article in the Treaty of Rome that gave the Commission trade-negotiating authority). While only the Commission negotiating team operates on the *external* front, for its negotiating mandate it must secure consensus in the 113 Committee, drawn from the senior bureaucracies of the member-states, or run the risk of turndown by the political-level Council of Ministers. Insofar as private-sector political pressures feed into policymaking, they operate more via the member-states than through ongoing consultative arrangements with the Commission. Indeed, Community-wide private-sector associations have tended to be weaker than their national counterparts because of internal conflict arising from differing national positions. That, of course, is changing under the impact of Europe 1992.

An interview with the president of the European Chemical Industry (CEFIC) in the *Financial Times* is revealing in this respect.[23] The chemical industry, he argues, has a clear long-term interest in preserving the multilateral trading system "even though it is currently more fashionable to concentrate on the single market," and ever since the Uruguay Round began, CEFIC has been actively engaged in lobbying with the Commission in Brussels. But "compared with the U.S., . . . whose elaborate system of consultation between private sector industry and officialdom allowed business a considerable say in the formulation of trade policy, it was much harder for European industry to make its influence felt." While chemical companies found it "easy to agree among themselves on the objective of liberal trade," other industries had more complex problems, and governments in Europe had "differing attitudes towards the GATT" so that political contacts were "of necessity fragmented." The CEFIC president said that while he understood the Commission's difficulties over agreeing to farm reform as part of the round, "agriculture should not be allowed to become a bottleneck. At some stage, too, private businessmen might need to develop a greater instinct for getting their views across, *with possibly more formalized arrangements for doing so*" (emphasis added).

The political economy of trade policymaking in the EC thus contrasts sharply with that of the United States. It is centered, internally, in the 113 Committee, on achieving a balancing of interests among member-states. The core of the mechanism is bureaucratic, with only infrequent trade ministerial input and no ongoing discussion of the broad trade policy thrust. As an internal bureaucratic mechanism it is extremely complex to operate effectively and requires considerable strategic and diplomatic skill on the part of the Commission negotiators, which they often put to good use in their external negotiations with the less "diplomatic" American activists. The private-sector input is still heavily weighted at the level of the member-state. At the Commission level, it is product-specific rather than broad-based.

One consequence of this political economy is a systemic bias to conservatism and inertia in high policy in the trade field: again, a marked contrast to the U.S. propensity to activism. (This inertial tendency was for a time exacerbated by the impact of Europe 1992, which forced the external policy implications to be made on the run, as it were.[24]) This systemic bias has been well described:

> Like the United States [policy], the trade policy of the European Community is made by compromises among strongly represented regional and industrial interests—but even more so. Given the need for compromise among member states, there is a tendency to agree on the lowest common denominator of protection. The allegedly more liberal countries then salvage their consciences by asserting that they are compromising their principles in favor of the still greater principle of European unity. The tendency to agree on protectionism is reinforced by the fact that decisions are ultimately taken in the Council of Ministers, which will consist of the industry or agricultural ministers directly concerned.
>
> Another consequence of the negotiating process is to externalize internal conflict. If, for example, the West German steel industry is hurt by subsidies from the Italian Government to Italian producers, the natural response is a combination of some limit on those subsidies with greater protection against outsiders. Furthermore, because of the nature of the European Community, it is only rarely that it can agree on any far-reaching initiatives in global arrangements, where the running has been left almost entirely to the United States. Finally, once reached it is only with great difficulty that a Community position can be modified.[25]

It is useful to compare this political economy of policymaking for the GATT round with that for Europe 1992. The divergence between the role of the major European corporations in the two high policy processes could scarcely be more marked. As will be more fully detailed in the next chapter, in Europe 1992, the multinational corporations—through their new organization, the European Roundtable (founded by Pehr Gyllenhammar, chairman and CEO of Volvo)—played a fundamentally important and leading role in the strategic formulation of the move to the internal market and have continued to do so as it has proceeded. This is, without exaggeration, an example of high policy activism that could hardly be matched anywhere else in the world. The combined efforts of an activist Commission and a unified activist business community overwhelmed the forces of conservatism and inertia. The image of "Europe Inc." is not too gross a caricature.

The creation of a new structure—the European Roundtable—involves costs, in time and effort (very costly at the level of the CEO of a global corporation), in funding a secretariat, and so forth. High policymaking is most effective when there is, indeed, a permanent organization. This will not usually be undertaken voluntarily without some reasonable expectation of return. That is why the number of broad-based business coalitions in the United States is, at least in part, a cultural artifact and why elsewhere a government-mandated structure may be the only way to overcome this impediment by, in effect, partly "taxing" the corporations and partly subsidizing the costs. It seems logical to argue, then, that in the case of the EC, the benefits that the key corporations saw in Europe 1992 were sufficiently large and meaningful in terms of their own corporate operations to overcome the reluctance to undertake the costs of building an ongoing, activist high policy coalition. It seems equally logical to argue that the same cost-benefit equation was not relevant in the case of the GATT round, because the corporations either saw little relevance in the negotiations to their most pressing concerns or, more likely, felt that the GATT was not an institution that could play any meaningful role in promoting their priority interests. They identify much more readily with either their national governments or, increasingly, the European Commission. (Of course, the same organizational capacity could have been used for both Europe 1992 and the Uruguay Round, but efforts in that direction have, so far, proved ineffectual.)

While this explanation for the divergence between the Uruguay Round and Europe 1992 in the political economy of high policymaking in Europe seems plausible, other factors are also probably at play. Firms may not act in their own self-interest if they lack information or suffer from myopia. Indeed, the Commission has made an effort to stimulate Roundtable interest in the Uruguay Round (a sign of a marked change in Commission policy concerning business participation[26] and, no doubt, a sign of the Commission's changing and more powerful role as a consequence of Europe 1992). After considerable effort, it arranged for the European Roundtable to visit Geneva in November 1988 so that the GATT secretariat and the ambassadors of a number of member-countries could brief members. By all accounts it was a worthwhile but rather disappointing event, if judged by the Roundtable participants' lack of information and interest in the GATT round. A similar effort, to bring business representatives to the Montreal Mid-Term Ministerial Meeting a month later, failed altogether. Yet the Commission seems hopeful that more information can stimulate greater interest, and it may well be that in the last year of the Uruguay Round, with the final ministerial meeting to take place in Brussels, the European business community can be persuaded to play a little more active role in the policy process.

Finally, it is worth noting, in the case of services and intellectual property—agenda items where the bottom-line losses are most evident to many large corporations (that is, the expected returns from an agreement would be more than sufficient to overcome the "transactions costs")—European corporations did cooperate in producing specific input to the Uruguay Round. But, as I have stressed already, this came about only as a result of American activism, including spelling out in hard figures the magnitude of loss from inadequate protection of intellectual property rights in many parts of the world.

Japan

If the main arena for intermediation, or brokering, in the trade policy system of the United States lies in the private sector–congressional interface and that of the EC in reconciling the positions of member-states, the Japanese system is primarily one of bureaucratic balancing among the major departments concerned—MITI; the Ministries of Foreign Affairs, Finance, and Agriculture; and the Economic Planning Agency—although others may be drawn in as appropriate, such as the Ministry of Posts and Telecommunications. However, more recently, this system of bureaucratic governance has also had to respond to politicians in both the cabinet and the Diet.[27] But such political input is less concerned with initiating or creating policies than with defending constituency interests where these overlap with sectoral interests, especially agriculture. It is thus product-specific rather than broad-based high policy. Essentially, then, the bureaucratic paradigm prevails in the high policy domain of the Uruguay Round.

The major bureaucratic tension in the GATT negotiations is that between the Ministry of Foreign Affairs and MITI, with the latter, for historic reasons, much more closely associated with industry. The intense bureaucratic rivalry and the need to achieve consensus before tabling a negotiating position in Geneva often produce a similar appearance of immobility to that of the EC, although for very different reasons.

The role of the private sector in the trade policy system of Japan again differs very markedly from that in the other two regions. Most ministries have legally mandated policy advisory committees or commissions. Indeed, there are 214 of these organizations! But they deal with a vast range of issues in addition to trade. They operate very differently from the U.S. committee structure in that the policy position, hammered out beforehand by the bureaucrats, is presented as more or less a fait accompli to the advisory committee (which is staffed by ministry officials) and is rarely subject to modification. More give-and-take (again largely on product-specific rather than generic policy issues) occurs at the level of the Zoku (Diet members who have policy expertise in specific areas).

In addition to this extremely elaborate, but largely ritualistic, internal committee structure, several new structures are specifically oriented to the Uruguay Round process. Thus the Ministry of Foreign Affairs has established an advisory committee for the GATT round, which includes business representatives; the Japan External Trade Organization (JETRO) has done the same; and MITI has committees on intellectual property and investment. The Keidanren, the most influential business coalition in Japan, is represented on all these advisory committees.

The Keidanren represents the largest companies in various industrial sectors, as well as in trading and finance. Traditionally, the coalition has been liberal and international in outlook, and its public statements have been strongly supportive of the Uruguay Round. It and other industrial groups have, for example, argued in favor of agricultural reform in Japan as essential to progress in the Uruguay Round. The Keidanren facilitated Japan's cooperation with the American-led effort in both services and intellectual property. It has also played a role in the Administrative Reform Council, which deals with structural issues that, although not directly linked to the Uruguay Round, are nonetheless trade-related and a source of continuing international friction.

Nevertheless, the main focus of the Japanese business community, even at the highest corporate level of the broad-based coalition, is *trade* rather than *trade policy*. And the core of the interface between government and business is also trade, not the high policy process of the Uruguay Round or, indeed, the low-track policy of trade remedy laws, which Japan scarcely uses.

The close and pervasive relationship between MITI and Japanese business began with postwar recovery, when an export orientation was essential to eliminate balance-of-payments constraints on growth and to expand and update domestic productive capacity. While, as the next chapter points out, this paradigm has changed in a number of respects over the past decade, and experts are by no means agreed about the role of MITI today,[28] the essential nature of the MITI-business interface remains qualitatively different from that of comparable relationships in the United States or Europe, with the possible exception of France (where the move from the mandarinate to business also tends to resemble the Japanese model).

The important characteristic of this difference is captured in the following summary of detailed case studies of how firms in different countries adapted to the upheaval in world petrochemical markets during the 1980s:

> The Japanese companies believe that it is helpful to have organizations such as MITI that use the best intelligence possible to provide a view of the industrial situation and powerful bureaucrats to negotiate with other ministries and the Diet. The bureaucrats at MITI believe that it is essential to have strong, independent private companies to develop and implement strategic plans. These beliefs contribute to the basis for a consensus-building process in which the companies accept an interference from, or a dependence on, the government that German, United Kingdom, and United States companies would find unacceptable.[29]

The Japanese model of the political economy of trade and industrial adjustment does on occasion extend to trade policy, not in the high policy process but in bilateral trade conflict. This is very evident in the U.S.–Japanese semiconductor dispute, where MITI has expended considerable effort to persuade Japanese companies to increase their use of foreign products. One analyst offers this insight into the different U.S. and Japanese paradigms:

> In March 1986, American and Japanese semiconductor manufacturers met in Los Angeles to discuss their disagreements related to international trade. The Japanese delegation included representatives from MITI. American government officials did not participate. S. Bruce Smart, the Under Secretary of Commerce for International Trade, stated that "we don't think we should put ourselves in the middle of private transactions, and secondly we were concerned that our presence there somehow would be interpreted as some form of repeal or absolution from antitrust laws."[30]

It should be added, however, that the U.S. government action was based on the effective lobbying of the American firms—the "special protection for special interests" model (see below).

To summarize, the political economy of high policymaking in Japan is largely directed to a product-specific orientation, although some developments have occurred during the Uruguay Round to encourage a broader-based focus. This provides a marked contrast with the United States, which paradoxically emerges with a unique "U.S. Inc." image. The political economy of trade and industrial development in Japan, which, as we will see, is more relevant to innovation policy, presents an equally stark contrast with the United States.

Before we turn to low-track trade remedy law, it is worth spelling out some of the implications of the striking asymmetry of high policy political economy in the Triad at this particular conjuncture in the international economy.

The American business community—and especially the activist corporations in broad-based coalitions, including the government-mandated advisory structure—has played an important role in the Uruguay Round negotiations, a role that in fact has extended to involving global corporations in both Japan and Europe on specific agenda items. This uniquely American thrust on high policy is a given: indeed, under the 1988 Omnibus Act the role of business is strengthened via the 301 processes. So, while the activist role of business in U.S. high policy is a given, its impact is not now clear. As American trade policy has become more complex, including some developments essentially at variance with basic GATT principles, it is difficult to forecast how strongly supportive of the Uruguay package the coalitions will be at the end of 1990 (especially when the product-specific lobbies are brought into play and a "coalition of the frustrated"[31] could bring together the losers to influence the deals that have to be made across sectors). At the same time, the U.S. administration has attempted to stave off some of the strong unilateralist tendencies by the traditional technique of assuring that particular problems will be dealt with in the Uruguay Round. This once-successful technique involves putting a great many eggs in the GATT basket and seems a far riskier course than it would have been in earlier, less-complex negotiations.[32]

In international terms, moreover, the risk is magnified. All the eggs are in the GATT basket, and the only activist participants in the Uruguay Round are the U.S. administration and U.S. corporations. The evident lack of intensive and continuing high policy participation by European and Japanese corporations stems, as we have seen, from a complex of historical, cultural, and institutional factors. It may also be based on an implicit assumption that, as has been true in the past, the Americans will take care of everything, so the EC and Japan might as well enjoy a free ride. This view may be changing in Japan, but thus far the evidence for that is not strong. In Europe the Commission is seeking more input from the European business community, with limited success to date. So even if the asymmetry narrows, and there is in the future some convergence on a more high policy-focused model, a fundamental mismatch in the political economy of policymaking in the Triad remains *at the present critical time*. And, as we will see in the next chapter, the mismatch is equally pronounced in the sphere of innovation policy.

LOW-TRACK POLICY: ANTIDUMPING

The distinction between high policy and low policy made at the outset of this chapter is convenient but not watertight. The low, or technical, policy track is the trade remedy laws that deal with protection against "unfair" trade (imports that are either subsidized by governments or dumped by private firms).[33] Along with safeguard action against serious injury from "fair" trade, these laws are often described as "safety valves," which, by providing relief or offset to industries injured by such imports, stave off demands for more sweeping protectionist action. But the trade remedy laws themselves are enacted by government and (as a form of high policy) can be changed so as to make protection easier to secure.

In the United States this has been, in fact, the price paid for liberalization in successive multilateral rounds. The trade remedy laws have become a kind of entitlement for American import-vulnerable industry. Further, in the United States, industries that are especially powerful in a political sense do not need to settle for using the trade remedy laws; they secure "special protection" through the executive branch, and this is reinforced by powerful congressional pressure. These "special deals for special cases,"[34] clearly high policy (if not in the edifying sense of that term), have covered textiles, autos, steel, and, most recently, semiconductors. On the other hand, in the EC, as we shall suggest, antidumping itself seems to be emerging, at least ex post, as a new policy instrument because of the degree to which officials can exercise discretionary authority under the regulations and procedures.

So, while the distinction between the two kinds of policy and the political economy of policymaking is still useful for analytic purposes, perhaps the key difference between high and low policy lies in the technical complexity of the trade remedy laws, which makes them virtually incomprehensible to the public or the politician and very much the domain of the administrator and the lawyer. Combined with this technical obscurity is the by no means obscure but rather politically powerful message of "unfair" trade.

The Tokyo Round ended in 1979. Between 1980 and 1987, over 1,200 antidumping cases and almost 500 subsidy–countervailing duty (CVD) cases were processed. In antidumping about half the cases were initiated by the United States and the EC; the other big users are Canada and Australia. In CVD, virtually all were American. There is little doubt that the trade remedy laws have become major policy tools. Antidumping regulation has now been adopted by 28 countries, including a number of developing countries, providing increasing opportunity to offset the structural adjustment liberalizing reforms of the World Bank.[35]

Further, while the original economic rationale for dumping was international price discrimination and predation, in practice dumping has been defined as sales below cost of production, which can rule out (or define as unfair) a good deal of normal business behavior sanctioned under domestic competition policy. This disparity between unfair and fair pricing in international as opposed to domestic law is especially marked in concentrated industries with rapid technological change and steep learning-by-doing cost advantages.

This discussion will be confined to antidumping, which is today the "weapon of choice."[36] Since the EC hardly uses CVD, and we want to compare the political economy of policymaking in the Triad, this is another reason to focus on antidumping. Japan has not employed either trade remedy law to any significant extent, although in recent years it has increasingly become the target for others. It will be interesting to see whether in the future some private-sector firms in Japan seek protection from unfair trade as imports from the NIEs continue to increase rapidly.

The trade remedy laws are triggered by industry and administered by the government bureaucracy. As mentioned, they are extremely complex and technical; in the United States and, increasingly, in the EC, their use requires the participation of highly sophisticated lawyers. A built-in momentum drives their rising frequency, as learning by doing generates more procedural expertise on the part of lawyers and more information by business on the opportunities the regulations afford.[37] The countervalence, which might be provided by consumers or users, is largely absent, not only from the administrative process, but also in political terms, since the procedures are often so tortuously technical as to be virtually incomprehensible to most of the news media.

In addition, because the nature of world trade is changing, and the GATT antidumping code is rather general and imprecise in a number of respects, the EC and, to a lesser extent, the United States have undertaken changes in antidumping laws, regulations, and administrative procedures that amount, in effect, to unilateral changes in the multilateral trade rules. These changes are directly affecting trade flows and, especially in the case of the EC, investment flows as well. Yet public awareness of the significant developments occurring in trade policy is low.

Because these developments differ in the EC and the United States it is useful to deal with each separately.

U.S. Antidumping

The origins of U.S. concern about dumping predate the GATT by decades: the Antidumping Act of 1921 was the basis for GATT article 6, which authorized antidumping duties. As part of the counterweight system to offset protectionist pressures on Congress—and thus avert specific legislative protectionist action—a set of "rules," or trade remedy laws administered by a quasi-judicial regulatory procedure, was designed. As I have pointed out, over time the trade remedy laws were changed so that enforcement was tightened and eligibility made easier. Indeed, this is a characteristic of trade remedy laws generally. Designed to protect against unfair trade by restricting imports, they facilitate lobbying pressure from those with an interest in protection, including "not only firms and industries beset by unfair competition, but more generally, those least favorably situated vis-à-vis their foreign competitors' costs."[38]

The U.S. system can be characterized as a bottom-up process—that is, initiated by private business and subject to no significant political or administrative discretion. Its administration is divided between two agencies—the International Trade Commission, which determines whether there is "material injury," and the Department of Commerce, which determines the dumping margin. While this division may be somewhat untidy and costly, it reduces the possibility of discretionary actions on the part of administrators. On the other hand, it prolongs the proceedings, and this may impose a severe burden in cases where no injury is found or where there is predatory intent on the part of the foreign firm.

The system is also relatively transparent for the parties involved in the proceeding and subject to broad judicial review. Both the transparency—the possibility of disclosure of confidential information—and the judicial review add an external check to administrative discretion. Indeed, the U.S. system provides little room for discretion, lacking a "public interest" standard as in the EC and Canadian laws.

In one area, however, the 1988 Omnibus Act has introduced discretion. This is the question of "circumvention" when producers of a product subject to antidumping duties undertake to avoid these duties by a variety of means—assembly of components, production in third countries, minor changes in the product, and so forth. The new amendment may open up discretion for the Department of Commerce to deal with "product shifting" and "country hopping," and how it will operate in practice remains to be seen. The important issue of circumvention features prominently in the EC, which has taken a different and very controversial approach, as we shall see.

In sum, then, the U.S. system is a quasi-judicial, rather transparent one that reflects largely the initiatives of the users—that is, the private-sector complainants. It has been described, rather accurately, as privatized trade policy. And it conforms to the pluralist activist U.S. paradigm.

In response to the increasing impact of antidumping penalties in the United States, the Pro Trade Group, a coalition of exporters, importers, manufacturers, distributors, and others, has proposed a number of modifications to tighten the law, largely because of increasing concern that "greater international interconnections today" because of both ownership and production "cause antidumping decisions to have wide repercussions for American business."[39] Another business coalition, ECAT, has also launched an initiative to develop a proposal for the Uruguay Round, arguing that "like an epidemic, a rash of antidumping statutes is being enacted abroad [that] unless modified will undercut trade liberalization efforts."[40] In both these instances the "final straw" was the 1989 ball bearings case, which covered a vast range of products, and hit a wide array of users—including major industries such as aircraft, automobiles, machinery, and electronics—with a costly increase in input prices.[41] However, in response to this anti-antidumping pressure, the Trade Reform Action Coalition, composed of almost 100 various metalworking, textile, and apparel associations, is coordinating a campaign to stave off efforts to weaken current antidumping laws.[42] The Semiconductor Industry Association is concerned that the law be more responsive to dumping in the high-technology sector and has submitted a proposal to that effect.[43] At this time, the outcome of all this activity in terms of the U.S. policy position on antidumping reform at the conclusion of the Uruguay Round is impossible to predict.

At the outset of this discussion I pointed out that in the United States, if an industry is politically powerful, it is often successful in moving from low policy to high policy, or "special protection." The most recent example in the antidumping area is the U.S.–Japanese Semiconductor Agreement of 1986, resulting from an initiative by a small firm (Micron) that eventually involved the giants of the industry, such as IBM and Texas Instruments. Unlike instances of "special protection" in the 1970s, which were traditionally defensive, the semiconductor case is the first example of "offensive" protection in a concentrated industry where technological change and dynamic "learning curve" economies are crucially important to gaining and maintaining competitiveness. The rationale for this "special deal" rested heavily on the argument that the semiconductor industry was "strategic" in both a military and an economic dimension, and therefore required a special arrangement (see chapter 3). As we shall see in the case of the EC, European business has made similar arguments, but instead of shifting to high policy (that is, political debate and decision), officials seem to have *adapted* the low-track policy for similar "strategic" purposes.

Finally, another important link between high policy and low policy in the United States is related to section 301 and especially super 301 of the 1988 Omnibus Act. CVD and antidumping regulations deal with specified unfair trade practices, although the GATT does not use the term "unfair"; rather, it specifies practices of dumping and subsidization under conditions of injury and spells out disciplines relating to these practices, as well as to countermeasures. In part, because of frustration with the implementation of existing trade remedy laws, and what the United States viewed as the increasing irrelevance of the GATT, the new direction of U.S. trade policy, as we have seen, introduces a very wide-ranging notion of unfairness that is unilaterally defined (that is, it is not in the General Agreement) and unilaterally administered.

Thus, section 301 defines three categories of unfair trade practices: *unjustifiable* (any act, policy, or practice that violates the international legal rights of the United States, including trade agreement violation); *unreasonable* (defined as an act, policy, or practice that, while not necessarily violating legal rights of the United States, is deemed to be unfair and inequitable—such as denial of fair and equitable market opportunities, export targeting, or foreign government toleration of "systematic anticompetitive activities"); and *discriminatory* (denial of most-favored-nation [MFN] treatment to U.S. goods, services, or investment).[44] And super 301 expands the idea of unfairness to include "generic" trade practices of a country that result in restricted U.S. access across the board.

Nor is this inflating notion of unfairness confined to the United States. The EC in 1984 adopted the New Trade Policy Instrument (as a response to section 301 of the 1974 U.S. Trade Act), providing strengthened procedures for responding to "illicit commercial practices" and for removing injury due to imports or suffered in export markets. It also aims to ensure "full exercise of the Community's rights with regard to the commercial practices of third countries"—a very broad objective that has yet to be fully spelled out in practice.

These developments raise real doubts about the conventional view of trade remedy laws as safety valves that operate to maintain a reasonably constant level of protection. More particularly, because the definition of unfair is so vague and so elastic, and because it is unilaterally interpreted, these new developments open the door to new forms of protection. They might better be described as trapdoors than as safety valves.

EC Antidumping

The role of the Commission in the EC antidumping system has been compared with that of an "examining magistrate," in contrast to the quasi-judicial mechanism of the United States.[45] The most important reason for this difference lies in the different degree of transparency of the two systems, specifically as it affects the disclosure of confidential information. Under American law, counsel for interested parties can obtain information submitted by other parties in the proceeding. In the EC only nonconfidential information is available to other parties, and the Commission has a good margin of discretion in determining whether information qualifies as confidential. As one analyst says:

> In the absence of a system of disclosure of confidential information, as is the case in the EEC . . . the investigating authorities are the only ones with access to the complete file. Non-confidential summaries are generally of limited value. This leads to parties shooting in the dark at each other and to the undesirable situation that in many cases there are no external checks on the investigators until it is too late, that is, in court.[46]

This relative lack of transparency has the consequence of providing much greater leeway for administrative discretion by the Commission. This leeway is further enhanced by a judicial review mechanism whereby the European Court of Justice has limited its scope of review to procedure and has eschewed economic substance. This is best captured by a typical quote of a Court judgment:

> In considering these (and similar) arguments where the Council or the Commission is required to appraise complex economic situations (as in an antidumping proceeding), the Court limits its review of such an appraisal to verifying whether the relevant procedural rules have been complied with, whether the facts on which the choice is based have been accurately stated and whether there has been a manifest error of appraisal or a misuse of powers.[47]

According to one author who has reviewed a number of Court decisions: "A serious limitation on the usefulness of Court appeals is the Court's increasing tendency to steer clear of any meaningful review of facts."[48]

These two factors—limited transparency and limited review—plus the preponderant role of the Commission (whereas in the United States two agencies are involved, the Commission investigates, establishes the facts, and determines dumping margins and injury) enlarge the room for discretion and limit countervalence in the system. The role of the Council of Ministers is, indeed, restricted primarily to "rubber stamping the proposals for definitive action submitted by the Commission." The Council has the power to enact legislation, but "the Commission plays an essential role in the EEC legislative process: amendments to the EEC Antidumping Regulations can be adopted by the Council only upon a proposal to that effect by the Commission."[49]

An interesting side effect of this combination of lack of disclosure of confidential information, limited judicial review, and concentration of authority in the Commission is the difference between the U.S. and EC calculations of dumping margins—a key, if formidably esoteric, element of the entire system. A full exposition of these differences would take us too far afield in this analysis, but what it all amounts to, in effect, is a much more marked tilt in EC practice toward finding dumping, particularly against firms from Japan and the Asian NIEs exporting new products, and especially in information technology, which requires substantial services ancillary to the sale—marketing, advertising, distribution.[50] These methodological developments, initiated by the Commission, were codified in an amendment to the regulations in July 1988.

That amendment provided another extension of EC antidumping, which also seems to be targeted at the same countries and products:

> The central point of the extension is that where the exporter bears the antidumping duty, an additional duty may be imposed to compensate for the amount borne by the exporter. The extension provides that any party directly concerned can initiate an investigation by presenting evidence to the Commission that the resale price to the first independent buyer has not increased by the amount of the duty. Hence the competitors in the Community of an exporter who has not raised his Community prices by the full amount of an antidumping duty can initiate an investigation; and the investigation is very likely to result in the imposition of an additional duty.... The measure affects only products that pay an antidumping duty. Thus it again bears with full force on the products from Japan and the Far East.[51]

Steps to ensure that an antidumping duty is borne by consumers presumably are designed to permit domestic industry to gain or maintain market share. Foreign firms that anticipate such action by a government will, of course, raise their prices in advance. Price rigidity, or even the formation of cartels, would seem to be a potential outcome of such a policy thrust.

In addition to these methodological developments—abstruse but powerful in impact—other significant changes have occurred in EC antidumping in the past few years. In response to the problem of "circumvention" of antidumping penalties against final products by assembly in Europe, the EC adopted an amendment in June 1987 to deal with so-called screwdriver plants to permit extension of antidumping penalties under specified conditions. These conditions are as follows:

- Assembly or production was carried out by a party that is related to or associated with any of the manufacturers whose exports of the like product are subject to a definitive antidumping duty.

- Assembly or production was started or substantially increased after the opening of the antidumping investigation.

- The value of parts or materials originating in the dumping country used in the assembly or production of such a product exceeded the value of all Community parts or materials by at least 50 percent. (What this amounts to is that if more than 60 percent of the parts originated in the dumping country, dumping will be found: 60 percent exceeds 40 percent by 50 percent.)

This provision extends the application of antidumping duties to imports of parts without any prior finding of dumping of the parts. Companies are interpreting the 60 percent rule of origin as a 40 percent local content rule, even though technically it is not. Within a few months, as numerous observers have noted, the Japanese-owned companies concerned began to increase their use of Community parts to meet or exceed the 40 percent "threshold" of Community-value components.[52]

But the repercussions of the screwdriver amendment did not stop there. U.S. semiconductor firms, which are major exporters to Europe, are feeling pressure from European buyers to expand production in Europe—already well serviced by U.S. semiconductor subsidiaries. The same pressures are inducing Japanese and Korean firms to invest in Europe.

There is, as the EC has repeatedly stated, no Community local content rule. The behavior of the firms is anticipatory, or perhaps (so the EC has argued) simply based on misinformation. But as the chairman of Intel has put it: "We have lost business already. . . . You can't pick up a piece of paper that says why Intel has got to manufacture in Europe. The rules don't exist. But customer concerns are driving important decisions right now."[53] In October 1989 Intel announced that it would establish a manufacturing plant in Ireland, its first in Europe.

In yet another development stemming from a rule of origin, the EC charged a Japanese photocopier manufacturer (Ricoh) with circumventing the payment of dumping duties imposed in February 1987 on direct exports from Japan by exporting to Europe from its California plant. Again, one might interpret this, however incorrect technically, as a foreign-determined U.S. local content decision. The required amendment to the rules of origin for photocopiers, to codify this administrative decision, was adopted in July 1989.

This new rule of origin is unusual, in that it takes a negative approach by listing the manufacturing operations that do *not* confer origin but provides no guidelines as to what operations do so. Since national customs officials are responsible for enforcement, if an exporter disagrees with the decision, he must first appeal to the national customs authorities and, if this fails, to the EC Court of Justice.

A number of other changes, or "clarifications," have occurred in rules of origin. Again, of particular significance have been those in the information technology area. In February 1989 the Commission announced a rule of origin for integrated circuits, which specified the country where the process of "diffusion" takes place as the determinant of origin. Once again, this was interpreted as a signal that the most significant technological process of manufacturing should be located in the EC and set in train a number of investment decisions by Japanese firms. Those U.S. subsidiaries in Europe that import circuits from plants in other parts of the world (where the diffusion process occurs) have also voiced concern that this is a signal of local content pressure,[54] although, in technical terms, it is just a clarification of a 1968 regulation defining a product's origin as where the "*last substantial process or operation that is economically justifiable was performed*" (emphasis added). Similar "clarifications" are expected on a number of other information technology products.

As the *Financial Times* has noted:

> The first phase in the E.C.'s debate about what constitutes a European product took place in the 10 years after the 1968 regulation was adopted, during which 11 individual product rules were drafted. These ranged from radios and televisions ... to eggs, textiles and ball bearings. Broadly, those are products whose origin needed clarification right from the start and so represent the setting in phase of the E.C.'s rules of origin regime.
> The current batch comes in response to circumstances that were much less obvious then, such as the growing trade frictions with Japan, the increasing complexity of ... electronic products and the trend for Japanese companies ... to move manufacturing plants nearer their main markets.[55]

But, of course, these technical decisions in antidumping are not affecting the Japanese alone. As is already evident, they are affecting trade and investment decisions over a far broader range of firms and industries. More generally, the degree of uncertainty generated by this regulatory activity has created, as one Brussels lawyer has stated, "the ultimate non-tariff barrier—the impossibility of planning."[56]

A basic problem is that rules of origin do not come under the GATT. Indeed, no meaningful international rules govern national decisions in this area. In 1973 the Customs Cooperation Council (CCC) adopted the Kyoto Convention, which laid down broad general principles for national origin systems but provided no dispute settlement mechanism and no procedure to review national practices. Moreover, some major trading countries (for example, the United States) have never accepted even the broad guidelines of the Kyoto Convention. The secretariat of the CCC has received no mandate from its member-states beyond that to compile compendiums of national regulations. Thus, the scope for discretion in the determination and application of rules is very broad. It is of interest that the United States and others have brought the issue to the GATT in connection with reform of the antidumping code in the Uruguay Round.

In summary, the EC system differs markedly from that of the United States in the scope for administrative discretion in the operation of antidumping regulation. However, signs indicate that some opposition has been developing within the European business community. The trigger for this was not the developments described above, but the pricing agreement with Japan on semiconductors.

The EC challenged the U.S.–Japanese Semiconductor Agreement of 1986 in the GATT. The panel found that the Japanese action was not consistent with GATT principles. In August 1989 the EC announced it had reached its own pricing agreement with Japan, which set floor prices covering not only 256K and one-megabit DRAMs but also the next generation of four- and sixteen-megabit chips—presumably in *anticipation* of dumping. This has caused increasing concern among users in the Community, perhaps generating offsetting pressure, as in the United States over the ball bearing case. However, as the *Economist* noted:

> Replying to the complaints of chip consumers, a senior Commission official argues that preserving a European base in semiconductor technology is important: "We need to do something or Europe will become dependent on outside producers."[57]

Similarly, in explaining the imposition of provisional antidumping duties on small-screen color television sets made in South Korea, a Commission press release in October 1989 stated that the damage imposed on domestic industry "threatens the present viability and future development of the whole Community television industry, and must be seen in the context of related technologies throughout the consumer electronics sector."[58]

It thus seems reasonably clear that, at least in part, the complex web of arcane calculations and regulations spun out over the past few years, by utilizing administrative discretion in the low-track policy of antidumping, is a form of high policy involving the Commission and firms in selected industries. As I will discuss in the next chapter, antidumping is one element of an emerging policy set called innovation policy.

CONCLUSIONS

This chapter has demonstrated the marked differences in the political economy of trade policymaking in the Triad. The asymmetry is unplanned, stemming from a variety of historical, institutional, and cultural factors. But policy process affects policy substance. The effects of the process are often unintended by either governments or corporations. But the unintended effects can be pervasive in their impact on the evolution of trade and investment flows. Finally, one trend that this exposition picks out is the growing importance of policy directed to high-technology industries. This is the subject of the following chapter.

3

INNOVATION POLICY

The emergence of a new policy term in the OECD countries—innovation policy—reflects the confluence of a number of domestic, international, and intellectual factors during the 1980s. While the term is now widely used,[1] the policy set that defines it is still vague, if not murky. This is not surprising, given the brief history, the extreme generality of objective (promoting innovation), and the provenance—the inherited mix of industrial, science, and technology policies of the 1970s. It is important to emphasize that innovation policy is not a given: it is a policy, or, more precisely, a policy set, in the making, focused on the promotion and adoption of new technology (that is, the commercial development of the fruits of basic research). Thus, however much the policy mix and institutional structure of industry vary from country to country, the government-corporate interface is an essential component.

This chapter will begin with a brief sketch of the economic background, international and domestic, that created the conditions for the initiation of a new policy focus in many industrialized countries. It will then briefly sketch out changes in the climate of ideas (in the discipline of economics) that also have influenced and will continue to help shape the evolution of innovation policy. Another major force at play, in both the United States and the EC, has been the "Japanese paradigm," which has acted, in some respects, as an exemplar for developments in the other two blocs of the Triad. Finally, I will attempt to spell out some of the international policy implications of these developments.

BACKGROUND

A striking feature of OECD policies beginning in the 1980s, repeatedly stressed by the G-7 and in other international forums, has been the emphasis on structural adjustment—sometimes termed the Ronald Thatcher revolution. The structural adjustment initiative, launched after the oil shock of 1979–80, reflected concern about the structural dislocation of the shock, layered on the declining productivity and high inflation of the 1970s. To complement the new "fight inflation first" macro orientation, a range of micro policies designed to improve the adaptability of markets was advocated and, to an extent varying among different countries, was adopted. An increasingly formalized surveillance mechanism monitors progress.[2]

The policy framework utilized has been centered on four areas: labor markets, financial markets, industrial adjustment policies, and public-sector issues. In each instance the thrust of policy proposals is toward enhancing market forces by reducing government intervention, deregulation, privatization, tax and social security reform, and other such factors. At the highest level of generality, the overriding principle of the policy framework has been to elevate the objective of efficiency in all policy design. It should be noted, however, that this commitment to markets that has been manifest in a number of new policies, especially in financial markets, has not extended to foreign trade. Nontariff barriers have continued to increase, and as we saw in the previous chapter, increasing use of antidumping regulations has, at the very least, not enhanced competition and price flexibility.

The structural adjustment theme was and is important in itself. While precise quantitative estimates of impact are extremely difficult to make, the general consensus is that the effects have been significant in improving growth and growth potential, especially in Europe. But in the present context, the significance of structural adjustment lies elsewhere. The emphasis on efficiency, market forces, adaptability, and the like has created a climate of opinion—a *policy ambience*—that is fundamentally inimical to the defensive, market-impeding industrial policies for ailing industries of the 1970s. This is not to say that all these policies have been eliminated, for such is not the case. But they are gradually being eroded, and the likelihood of erecting new subsidy schemes and so forth for "sunset" industries is diminishing. The emphasis, instead, is shifting to competitiveness and high-technology sectors. A major reason for the shift lies in the international arena.

The rapid expansion of world trade in the past few decades has both fueled and been stimulated by world growth. Growth has, in other words, become steadily more trade-intensive. At the same time, an increasing number of countries are now participating in a world trading system embracing an ever-widening range of products. It was both these phenomena—the increasing importance of trade to sustained growth and improved living standards, and the rapid rise of new actors on the world scene—that prompted a mounting preoccupation among a number of OECD governments with technological change and competitiveness.

In more precise terms, the concern, which began in the 1970s, has stemmed both from the rise of the NIEs (whose share of OECD total manufacturing imports rose from 4 percent in 1973 to 8 percent in 1985 and, in the case of labor-intensive products, from 8 percent to 20 percent over the same period) and, especially, from the impressive success of Japan in many high-technology sectors, as may be seen in Figure 2. In both the NIEs and Japan, the idea has taken hold that performance is due to "created" comparative advantage. And at the heart of that issue has been the role of technological change and innovation.

Another international development of the 1980s has also prompted a higher profile for competitiveness questions and thus influenced the development of innovation policy: the global current account imbalances. This is particularly apparent in the United States. As a number of analysts have emphasized,[3] the required correction in the U.S. external deficit will involve not only macro policy (the fiscal deficit) but, at the micro level, an ongoing restructuring in the American economy. As the trade account improves, much of the increment in exports must come from increased manufacturing, and it is within the context of this American "reindustrialization" process that the competitiveness and innovation policy issues are highlighted.

In summary, domestic and international economic forces have coincided over the past decades to create a powerful mo-

56 □ INNOVATION POLICY

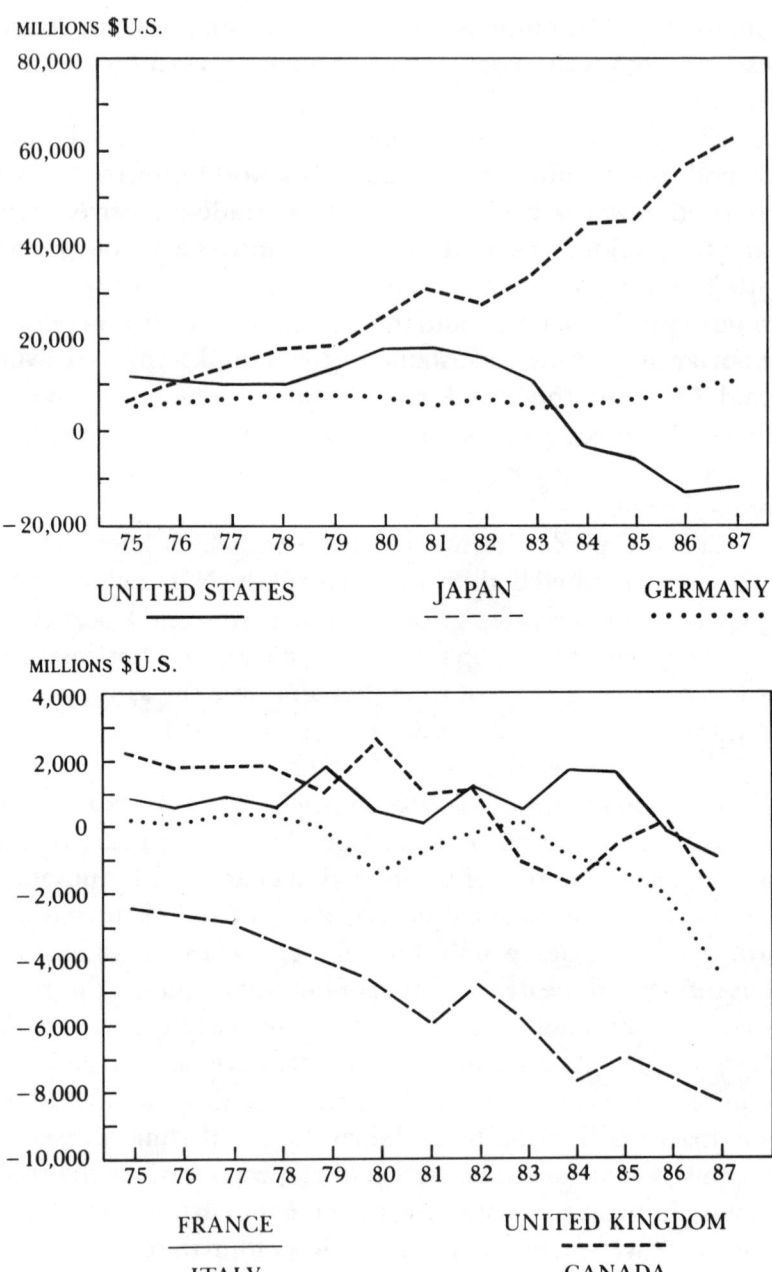

Source: OECD, *Industrial Policy in OECD Countries, Annual Review 1989* (Paris 1989).

FIG. 2. TRADE BALANCES OF HIGH-R&D-INTENSITY INDUSTRIES, 1975–1987, *millions of $U.S.*

mentum for a new policy orientation in the industrialized countries. Since the 1970s, the center of gravity of the industrial policies has shifted from ailing industries toward a new policy set directed to improving international competitiveness—innovation policy. Developments in the discipline of economics have also influenced this shift.

The Climate of Ideas

In what has become an oft-quoted passage in the *General Theory*, Keynes asserted:

> the ideas of economists and political philosophers, both when they are right and when they are wrong, are more powerful than is commonly understood.... I am sure that the power of vested interests is vastly exaggerated compared with the gradual encroachment of ideas.[4]

Whether it is the "power" of these ideas or simply the fact that they provide intellectually respectable backing for policies that governments and others want to undertake on their own grounds, a number of recent developments in economics have led to new arguments for government intervention in both trade and industrial policy. In the history of economic doctrine and economic policy, the role of the state has moved from the prescribed "nightwatchman" of Adam Smith, to the "nanny" of the postwar cradle-to-grave welfare state, to the "nemesis" of Ronald Thatcherism in the 1980s. Today, in the context of the debate over the sources of long-run competitiveness, the climate of ideas about the role of government seems to be shifting once again, or at least becoming more *nuanced.*

One strand of argument for new activist policies stems from the so-called new international trade theory.[5] A number of reasons that may explain the changes in international trade theory have been well reviewed in the rapidly expanding literature. Major contributing factors were developments in the nature of the trading environment—the increasing importance of trade among industrialized countries in technologically sophisticated products manufactured by large firms operating in imperfectly competitive markets—and changes in the economics discipline itself, in the theory of industrial organization. Changes in the nature of trade had, over a number of years, led to adaptation of the classical doctrine of free trade, which had been based on country-specific fixed endowments, unchanging technology, and perfect competition. The new literature simply extended the postwar theory of commercial policy. Developments in industrial organization and game theory have provided the requisite new tools for analysis and policy formulation.

In the literature, the basic idea is that for large countries, the presence of imperfectly competitive markets—with large, technologically sophisticated firms; economies of scale; heavy R&D costs; and dynamic learning advantages—provides a rationale for governments to act in favor of their domestic firms at the cost of foreigners. The rationale boils down to two aspects of such industries: "rents," in the form of higher profits or higher wages, and "externalities" (that is, benefits that spread beyond the firm itself to other firms or industries) from the high R&D expenditure. The argument goes that the government can take action in a variety of ways on behalf of its own firms by affecting the behavior of foreign firms or governments. (These measures are somewhat confusingly called "strategic" in the new theory; this usage should be distinguished from the more common one, denoting commercial or security aspects of leading-edge sectors.) Such action can result in higher profits or wages (and hence, possibly, higher tax receipts) or enhanced competitive advantage vis-à-vis other countries in certain industries or sectors.

These policy proposals have attracted growing criticism: clearly economists have reached no new consensus.[6] Analysts have criticized the proposals for an activist predatory trade policy based on capturing a larger share of the rents of oligopolistic industries as being too assumption-dependent, being too complex, and requiring too much detailed information for governments to handle effectively. All the old criticisms of the "picking winners approach apply to these new arguments for protectionism. Most forcefully (especially in the United States, given the nature of its political process), this criticism includes the danger that governments may fail to pick the right winners, but losers can be very skillful at picking governments. The United States may well have a comparative disadvantage in this respect vis-à-vis both the EC and Japan.

This debate may have weakened the rent-shifting argument for aggressive trade policy, but, in the context of the present discussion of innovation policy, the externalities argument has proved a more robust rationale for industrial policy advocates. Its proponents hold that such policies need not involve picking winners, in the sense of individual firms, but rather can focus on sectors and generic technologies, and are thus less information-intensive in policy formulation.

The externalities rationale is certainly more acceptable politically, which is important. It involves the highly visible issues of technological change, innovation, and competitiveness. It provides a justification for intervention not to benefit individual firms or groups of workers (which, as suggested, sounds just like old-fashioned protectionism in trendy garb), but to benefit whole industries or even the whole economy. Yet, potentially the most politically powerful argument—which contrasts with the neat, clear dictum derived from the liberal trade model—is that if other governments are pursuing such policies, then doing nothing at all risks the worst possible outcome. The industrial policy advocates are largely silent on systemic implications, which provide the most powerful counterargument to this increasingly seductive view. They have encountered strong criticism for ignoring the possibility of retaliatory cycles and the destabilization of the entire system.[7] But the traditional charge of many economists that externalities are the last refuge of the scoundrel (that is, interventionists)—or, as some have suggested, the first refuge—has never proved compelling to most policymakers.

The externalities argument is certainly not new and is not in theoretical terms associated with imperfect competition, although its relevance in this context is clear enough, since heavy R&D costs are a feature of modern, high-technology industries and often form an effective fixed-cost entry barrier. The presence of large externalities has long provided an intellectually respectable rationale for government intervention in basic R&D where private firms have little incentive to invest because the benefits cannot be fully captured in profits (appropriated). Thus a gap separates private and social returns to such investment (called an externality), and a logical case emerges for the government to step in. The new arguments for innovation policy center not solely on basic research but on the so-called middle ground between basic research and proprietary technology, usually involving cooperative arrangements between firms and government.

One continuing issue of dispute in the literature is the extent to which the externalities generated by government-sponsored R&D diffuse internationally. This is especially pertinent today in the light of the extensive network of R&D linkages being established by both corporations and research institutions. If the benefits of government-subsidized R&D in country A spill over to countries C, D, and E, the case for intervention is greatly weakened: any country can get a free ride by importing the new technology. But industrial policy advocates often add another argument: the "first-mover advantage" that a country or firm captures by preempting foreign rivals. This advantage provides the opportunity for firms and countries to consolidate and extend their competitive advantage.

Thus, while the debate is by no means settled, the tilt of the activist school of trade and industrial policy is centering on the technology/externalities, and "first-mover," rationale. This rationale proposes the following definition of "strategic" industries or sectors: those that generate significant externalities across a wide spectrum of industries in the home market and for which an exploitable advantage by a foreign firm or another country could have serious and widespread consequences.[8] Empirical verification and analysis will be very difficult and leave plenty of room for controversy.

In sum, recent developments in economics are creating a new climate of ideas, which is eroding the orthodoxy concerning the role of markets versus governments, in both trade and industrial policy, for leading-edge, high-technology industries. There is no longer a "rebuttable presumption" of national gains from trade liberalization: empirical verification from varying quantitative models is required. According to one expert: "We can draw an important conclusion about imperfectly competitive environments. From a national viewpoint, it is necessarily an empirical question whether there are gains from trade liberalisation or losses, gains from active trade intervention or losses."[9]

Finally, trade theorists have always understood that domestic policies can restrict trade: even the GATT endorses this view in, for example, the subsidy code and the principle of national treatment. But the clear, clean, normative rule that trade policy is a "second-best" instrument for correcting domestic market distortions and therefore a costly form of intervention has now been undermined.[10] Countries must be concerned not only with other countries' trade policies but with the international impact of many of their domestic policies. That this has long been the case in the real world, as the following discussion on Japan makes abundantly clear, fortifies the political appeal of this case.

INNOVATION POLICY IN THE TRIAD

The difficulty of coming to grips with a neat and unambiguous definition of innovation policy stems from the fact that a wide range of public policies, both macro and micro, affect the generation and application of new technologies. Two basic models summarize the essential nature of innovation policy strategies.[11] One seeks to push forward the technological frontier by developing leading-edge techniques, and the other centers on closing the gap between the actual and the best available practice by fostering technology diffusion.

While most countries engage in both types of policy, the tilt in the United States is "mission-oriented"—that is, concerned primarily with pushing out the technological frontier. Diffusion—that is, U.S. firms' process of adopting "best practice"—is less a conscious strategy than a by-product of the high internal mobility and openness of the American industrial and education system.[12] This makes the American system uniquely porous in *international* diffusion as well. Many European countries (Germany, Sweden, and Denmark, for example) have concentrated on policies and institutions devoted to effective domestic diffusion. Among the industrialized countries, only Japan has an innovation policy that explicitly includes and explicitly coordinates both mission- and diffusion-oriented objectives. As for the EC, in contrast to its individual member-countries, the policy stance is in a process of evolution but has borrowed elements of the Japanese model.

The Japanese Paradigm: The Exemplar

The effectiveness of the Japanese model in improved competitiveness and growth has been the subject of a vast outpouring of analysis.[13] A key issue in the literature has been the notion of targeting particular sectors and technologies. A number of questions about targeting have arisen in an increasingly insistent fashion, especially in the United States, as concern about slippage in leading sectors has mounted.[14] Does Japan target? What policies are involved? Was targeting a key element in Japan's outstanding growth and trade performance? What should be the policy stance of Japan's trading partners? Early in the 1980s the debate centered on "trade impact," the "asymmetry of access" to the Japanese market. While, as we have seen, that is still an (unsettled) issue, the targeting debate has widened to the all-embracing concept of policies designed to create competitive advantage.[15]

In the very nature of things, the debate about Japanese targeting will remain unsettled. It would require "evidence" about what the Japanese economy would have been in the absence of what was a unique and complex form of industrial policy. Since such evidence cannot exist, equally expert observers have arrived at widely disparate judgments—not usually about the *facts* of Japanese industrial policy, but about its *impact* on Japan and the international economy.

Another reason for continuing dissent on the evaluation of Japanese targeting is that significant changes have occurred in policy and players in Japan over the past decade, and, indeed, a process of evolution is still under way. Case studies of specific sectors—computers and semiconductors—document a pervasively interventionist policy mix in the 1950s and 1960s, orchestrated largely by MITI, but also involving the Ministry of Finance and other government departments as required. Designed to influence the industrial pattern of investment, the pragmatic and eclectic policy array included direct and indirect subsidies, trade protection, technology transfer, targeted R&D programs, and an array of market structure policies. The strategy had a number of important, indeed unique, features. These included the close and continuing cooperation between government (mainly MITI) and industry; the enunciation of long-term strategic goals (the MITI "visions") that were designed to and did influence firms' decisions on investment, marketing, skill training, and R&D; the use of organized market *structure* rather than *markets*, as in the United States, as a policy tool to effect diffusion, risk sharing, and market access; and the extent and nature of coordination of macro and micro policies to achieve a unique "climate-style" policy designed to affect broad forces such as savings, overall risk, and profits.[16]

The idea of Japanese industrial targeting during the rapid growth period of the 1950s and 1960s has assumed mythic proportions in some quarters. The myth is of a grand overall strategic design in which every outcome was carefully planned and successfully implemented. It is, of course, unwise to underestimate the power of myths! But, as several analysts have argued, some elements of Japanese policy were adopted to overcome basic deficiencies and distortions in domestic markets that the government was unwilling or unable to tackle head-on. And in many cases MITI picked losers. Further, as is not unusual, sometimes the unintended consequences of a policy overwhelmed the explicit objective. A good and much-discussed example of this is the effect of "reverse engineering," which was induced by the policy of licensing foreign technology rather than importing it through foreign direct investment, as in Canada and other countries in the earlier part of this century. Particularly in the auto industry, reverse engineering, together with the inherited *keiretsu* structure (conglomerate industrial groupings of companies, often including banks as well as producers, users, and distributors), played a major role in developing Japanese prowess in manufacturing processes. Fortuitous or planned? Maybe both. Nevertheless, it remains true that Japanese industrial policy during this period was significantly different from that of other industrialized countries in the degree to which conscious, designed, focused government intervention played a significant role (and a strikingly successful one, in terms of growth objectives).

From the mid-1970s, a number of changes occurred in the industrial policy mix. International pressure and the Tokyo Round of GATT negotiations resulted in significant trade liberalization, which continued into the 1980s. Fiscal deficits, and financial market deregulation in the 1980s (induced by both domestic and international forces), reduced the scope and impact of the financial measures that had been used in the earlier period to influence the rate of growth and the allocation of investment. More recently, fiscal expansion and the high yen have brought about further change, expanding domestic demand and increasing imports, especially from the NIEs. In addition, the growing financial strength and global span of Japanese corporations has made them less willing to accept "guidance" from government bureaucrats. Moreover, the "technology gap" between Japan and the United States had narrowed or closed in many sectors, and this in itself required a shift in a strategy originally geared to catch-up. While all these changes—many of which, like financial market deregulation, are still ongoing—have certainly altered the means by which Japan's industrial or innovation policy is implemented, the policy remains unique in a number of respects, both in its effective combination of mission-oriented and diffusion strategies, and also in its singular blend of cooperation, competition, and shared information and objectives.

Certainly the changes of the past decade have not quelled the ongoing debate about Japanese targeting. On the contrary, as I have said, the debate has heated up and has included the charge that Japanese targeting creates a built-in tendency to surplus capacity and hence to dumping in periods of declining demand. One very important new development of the 1980s has been the reaction of policymakers in the other two blocs of the Triad to the Japanese innovation policy model.

The United States: In Transition

In the U.S. mission-oriented model, government resources dedicated to pushing out the technological frontier have been heavily concentrated on defense and space. This characteristic is one the United States shares with other countries—for example, France and the United Kingdom. But the U.S. innovation system is sui generis in several respects: its size, diversity, flexibility, and porousness are unmatched. In marked contrast to the focused Japanese paradigm, the U.S. model is pluralist and marketlike, fueled by competition and mobility between and within the three nodes of the research system: industry, universities, and government. Indeed, it is only in defense and space programs that the concept of a top-down government strategy involving explicit long-term objectives and policy instruments is appropriate. And even there, the mission-oriented programs of the United States are characterized by their fragmentation and diversity.

What is often overlooked in discussions of U.S. innovation policy is the sheer absolute size of private-sector R&D expenditure. Thus in 1987, expenditure by the business sector on R&D in the United States was $84.6 billion (over half the total business expenditure on R&D in the OECD), dwarfing the Japanese figure of $30.4 billion and the German $16.9 billion (all in current purchasing power parity estimates).[17] American industry not only is the chief agent for converting technical change into economic use in the United States, but, in the 1960s and 1970s, it provided a "role model" for corporate behavior in the other industrialized countries. Thus, while industrial research originated not in the United States but in the German chemical industry in the late nineteenth century, the uniquely American contribution that evolved in the 1950s was "the deliberate, planned use of R&D as a mechanism for corporate growth."[18] Europe and Japan copied this over the next two decades, but U.S. industry had an important head start of ten to fifteen years. However, by the late 1970s, in a number of sectors, both intensified competition and accelerating technological change were placing the technical resources firms needed to remain active global players beyond the capacity of a large number of individual corporations. The forces of technology itself required change in the model.

One response to these new pressures has been an adaptation of *corporate* organization and strategy to create worldwide technical links through subsidiaries, joint ventures, strategic alliances, and so on. And given the nature of the American system, new forms of university-industry linkage have also become increasingly important.[19]

Other developments in the 1980s, partly in response to these underlying technological and economic forces, but also stimulated by the Japanese targeting issue, were several significant changes in U.S. *government* policy. These have been largely ad hoc and responsive. They do not add up to an overall, planned change in strategy, and the debate about U.S. innovation policy remains both divisive and unsettled.

The first significant change of the decade was the 1984 passage of the National Cooperative Research Act (NCRA), designed to encourage cooperative research among firms, and thereby encourage sharing of cost and risk along the lines of the Japanese model, by providing some limited exemption from antitrust legislation.[20] As one expert notes, "a direct response to Japanese government policies favouring cooperative research in precompetitive, 'generic' technology was the formation of the Microelectronics and Computer Technology Corporation (MCC) in January 1983,"[21] and it was this and similar private-sector initiatives that prompted the 1984 law. Since the passage of the act, a number of cooperative research projects have been established, but in the highly competitive U.S. milieu, considerable tension is evident between the dual objectives of cooperation and competition—a tension so effectively brokered by MITI in the Japanese model.

Perhaps the most important venture established to date under the new policy on market structure was Sematech. A Defense Science Board report in February 1987 warned that the U.S. military's growing reliance on imported foreign semiconductor chips was a potential national security risk and recommended establishing and funding a central facility to produce DRAM chips.[22] The proposal actually adopted in December

1987 came from the semiconductor industry; it is a joint enterprise between the government (Defense Department) and industry to develop new production processes for use in manufacturing semiconductors—that is, precompetitive generic research on the Japanese model. (Another, quite different, initiative, which would likely require antitrust clearance if and when established, is U.S. Memories. In June 1989 IBM and six other American electronic companies announced plans to establish U.S. Memories for joint production of DRAMs. The project would likely not be eligible under the 1984 act, which deals with research, not manufacturing, joint ventures.)

The 1984 change in U.S. antitrust law was modest and, in the view of many industry spokespersons, represented only the first step in what is regarded as a need for more significant reform. Thus, according to two analysts, changes in antitrust law are required "to facilitate a more rapid response by American 'high technology' industries or product groups to competitive challenges, because firms would have available a richer variety of organizational mechanisms and resources to respond to targeting strategies from abroad." They argue that U.S. antitrust law was developed for stable, concentrated industries, operating in largely domestic markets, and thus imposes "unnecessary restrictions on high technology industries . . . [which] are practically immune from the potential for cartelization because of uncertainties generated by domestic and international competition."[23]

The question of antitrust reform is highlighted here because it signals the much broader issue of market structure as a key element in the innovation process and therefore in innovation policy. A great deal has been written about the significance to Japanese innovation policy of the *keiretsu*.[24] While historically based, this singular form of market structure has also been a designed outcome of government policy. Especially in the earlier period, sculpting market structure and fine-tuning performance was a central element in Japan's industrial policy. In striking contrast, the only American policy instrument directed explicitly to market structure is antitrust. In fact, vigorous suits concerning AT&T's Bell Laboratories and IBM during the 1950s played a major—if largely unintended—role in stimulating semiconductor and computer innovation. The important question is whether these recent developments in the application of U.S. antitrust law, largely an ad hoc response to a particular aspect of the Japanese innovation model, are the beginning of a more significant redefinition of market structure policy in the United States.

Another significant aspect of the NCRA-Sematech development is the evolving role of the Department of Defense. As the size and even the direction of spillover between military and civilian technologies have changed, so has the nature of the Defense Department's role in financing technological research. The Defense Advanced Research Projects Agency (DARPA) has become highly visible (labeled hyperbolically "America's Answer to Japan's MITI" by *The New York Times*)[25] as the sponsor not only of Sematech but also of, for instance, the National Center for Manufacturing Sciences (NCMS), the Superconductivity Competitiveness Initiative, and high-definition television. In all these projects military funding is based on two assumptions: "(1) technological spillovers in process and product technologies and design now flow primarily from commercial to defense applications in this sector; and (2) U.S. suppliers of defense technologies cannot survive without maintaining a strong presence in commercial markets."[26]

The changing role of the Department of Defense has become a part of the ongoing debate in the United States over innovation policy, with proponents of a more active approach arguing for the establishment of a civilian agency in the Department of Commerce and opponents of industrial policy seeking to diminish DARPA's funding. Be that as it may, the new orientation of Defense has potentially important international implications. Indeed, these are already apparent. Thus, "the provision of the NCMS charter that restricts the international transfer of technologies . . . could hamper the ability of U.S. multinationals to manage international R&D operations."[27] The same restrictive provision applies to the superconductivity initiative. Sematech has excluded U.S. subsidiaries of foreign firms.

As mentioned in the previous chapter, another important development in U.S. policy in the 1980s, which is linked to the innovation issue, was the semiconductor arrangement between the United States and Japan. The U.S.–Japanese Semiconductor Agreement of July 1986 followed a series of legal actions on dumping initiated by U.S. semiconductor firms. In the lead-up to the agreement the Semiconductor Industry Association (SIA) had argued in a series of reports that Japanese dumping is a result of Japanese targeting which, by creating overcapacity, threatens strategic sectors of the American economy.

The Semiconductor Trade Agreement on DRAMs was unusual in a number of respects. As already noted, it prohibited dumping not only in the U.S. market but also in third-country markets by requiring MITI to operate a minimum export price system. In addition, the agreement provided for opening Japanese markets. The precise wording was that the Japanese government should provide "substantially improved opportunities for foreign semiconductor sales in the Japanese market more reflective of the competitiveness of the U.S. industry." The 1986 foreign market share in Japan was just over 10 percent, mostly American. The Americans have argued (and the Japanese have denied) that the understanding was more precise than this: that the U.S. share was expected to increase to 20 percent of the Japanese market by 1991, the terminal date of the arrangement. This difference in view generated considerable acrimony. By April 1987, the foreign share had shrunk to about 8.5 percent, and amid mounting complaints about Japanese targeting and unfair trade practices and concerns about U.S. security spelled out in the Defense Science Board's February report, the administration imposed tariffs on $300 million of Japanese consumer electronics. The administration described the sanctions as largely "symbolic"—a strategic threat to compel compliance with the agreement—and they were partly lifted a few months later. By 1989, after a variety of MITI-organized industry initiatives, U.S. market share had scarcely changed, evoking demands for renewed and more extensive sanctions. As the 1991 expiration date of the agreement approaches, political pressure will again mount for some form of trade policy response.

Without going into a detailed account of the impact of the bilateral agreement on the American semiconductor industry, it is worth noting that the evidence suggests it may well have accelerated Japanese and other Asian competitors' entry into the more sophisticated sectors of the industry now dominated by the U.S. firms.[28] This is a familiar story: the extra profits that accrued because of the pricing agreement are being deployed to improve Japanese competitiveness in sectors where they are relatively weak.

The significance of the agreement in the current context is not simply that it was a precursor of the new unilateralist direction in U.S. trade policy codified in the 1988 act, but that it represented the first "special case" based on a strategic (in commercial and security terms) industry rationale.

Thus, the trade and market structure policy developments of the 1980s in the United States were closely linked, and both represented a response to the Japanese innovation policy paradigm.

EC: Strategic Reach

Although R&D expenditures at the national level in Europe far outweigh those of the Community, marked changes, centered on information technology, occurred in EC innovation policy in the 1980s. These changes point to a new approach in R&D policy and, as we saw in the previous chapter, a trade policy element (antidumping) is emerging, as it were, out of the closet. Further, the Commission's mandate to coordinate trade, competition, and technology policies was fully clarified and legitimated as the European Technology Community and incorporated into the Single European Act. It has now been endorsed at the highest levels of European industry, most explicitly in the information technology field.

The specter haunting Europe in the early 1980s was fear of declining competitiveness vis-à-vis the Americans and especially the Japanese. The Europessimism was concentrated on the information technology industries, and here the preoccupation was with Japan. The Japanese announcement of the Fifth Generation Program in 1981 had a major and immediate effect in stimulating national government action in the computer field; Britain's Alvey program in 1982 and France's much larger Filière Electronique R&D program the same year were launched as a direct response. Private firms also began other pan-European projects.[29] (As an expert in computers remarked to me privately, the Fifth Generation Program had a greater impact on foreign governments than on the Japanese computer industry!)

It was against this background that Viscomte Davignon, EC commissioner for industry and (after 1982) for research and technology, established the Information Technology Industry Roundtable, made up of representatives of the twelve largest electronic firms in Europe: AEG, Nixdorf, and Siemens of Germany; Thompson, Bull, and CGE from France; Olivetti and STET from Italy; Philips from the Netherlands; and ICL, GEC, and Plessey from the United Kingdom. As one commentator explained: "His aim was to establish a MITI-type programme of collaborative R&D to be called ESPRIT—European Strategic Programme for Research in Information Technology—something the Commission had actually been trying to get off the ground since the mid-1970s but which had, until Davignon's initiative . . . fallen on deaf ears."[30] By December the Commission had the approval for a modest pilot jointly funded by industry and the Community, to last through 1983. This was followed by the first phase, from 1984 to 1988. The second phase of ESPRIT began in 1989.

ESPRIT became the model for subsequent programs in information technology, so it is worthwhile spelling out its main features:

- It was jointly funded by government (the Commission) and industry.

- It targeted precompetitive research projects selected by joint teams of bureaucrats (many on secondment from industry) and industry specialists.

- It provided a channel of continuing communication and cooperation among European firms (many of which already had established licensing or distribution arrangements with U.S. or Japanese firms, but not with other Europeans).

- It created, by its institutional structure, a set of common views about the evolution of technology and markets at the top level of the dominant European enterprises. These common views were intended to influence the firms' long-term investment decisions. According to one expert, "The VLSI [Japanese Very Large Scale Integrated Circuit] and Fifth Generation Programmes are based on this principle (that is, common views about the future); MITI effectively acts as a mechanism which ensures that all firms act on a common set of expectations. . . . In the case of ESPRIT, Davignon's Round Table fulfilled this same function."[31]

- Most important of all, perhaps, was the success of ESPRIT not simply in its projects, but in fostering and reinforcing the emerging new confidence and determination that pan-European cooperation was the only way to restore competitiveness vis-à-vis the Japanese and Americans.

The specter of Europessimism was replaced by the exciting vision of Europe 1992. Another business organization—the European Roundtable—provided a new and very important channel of communication and cooperation among the top levels of leading European firms, and between industry and the Commission. While, of course, many factors influenced the adoption of the Single Market policy, the role of business was key, and for European industry (at least for the major European corporations) the issue of technology and competitiveness was the sine qua non.

A speech given by Wisse Dekker, the head of Philips, in 1985, just a few months before the Commission issued its *White Paper* on the internal market, is noteworthy in this respect. For Dekker, the essence of the internal market rested on its effects on Europe's competitive position because "economies of scale are needed to cover the gigantic rise in research and development costs which are characteristic of modern technology and which exceed the scope of national markets. . . . Economies of scale and speed of growth are also the strategic elements used by our competitors world-wide."[32]

The size of the EC's technology projects—the largest are Research in Advanced Communication Systems for Europe (RACE) and Basic Research in Industrial Technologies for Europe (BRITE)—is still dwarfed both by member-states' expenditure and by American and Japanese government R&D subsidies. But the significance of the Commission mandate (to coordinate technology, trade, and competition policies) and of the ESPRIT-model of industry-government, long-view targeting is far greater than that of expenditure in pointing a direction for EC innovation policy evolution.

Instructive in this respect is the 1989 development, the Joint European Semiconductor Silicon Project (JESSI), which is an offshoot of Eureka. Eureka was a 1985 French-inspired answer to the American request for European cooperation in the Strategic Defense Initiative, and is open to some European countries outside the Community. JESSI could just as well have come under ESPRIT, so it provides a good example of the current innovation policy approach.

JESSI is a far more ambitious project than ESPRIT and its offshoots, in terms of funding, coordination span, and scope. According to the pamphlet prepared by the JESSI Planning Group, the overall objective of the project is "to secure Europe's long-term share of the world market for micro-electronics" by reducing European dependence on imports of semiconductors and other products, such as production equipment. The target is the next generation of memory and logic devices. Thus the group notes:

> Two thirds of all IC's [integrated circuits] in European products come from the U.S.A. and Japan. Moreover, European IC manufacturers rely a great deal on Japanese and American production equipment. A dangerous situation, as free access to the most modern products and technologies can be cut off at any moment: by the U.S.A. for national security, by Japan for economic reasons.[33]

Similar in intent to the U.S. Sematech, JESSI is, however, far more heavily funded and much less narrowly focused, covering both supplier and user industry technologies. As Robert Noyce, head of Sematech, aptly put it, JESSI is "covering the waterfront with everything from fibre optics to high-definition television to communications."[34] As is the case with Sematech, foreign subsidiaries are excluded from membership.

JESSI is not confined to new technology in the production of semiconductors, but is aimed at microelectronics as a broad sector and at Japan. The JESSI Planning Group clearly states:

> The Japanese aim to become world leaders in micro-electronics. Government and firms again and again focus great efforts directly on a particular segment of the world market. For video recorders, cameras and hi-fi systems, they have already achieved their goals. What's more, for years Nippon Telegraph and Telephone has been involved in chip research programmes of billions of US dollars per annum, the results being made available to their industry. Thus within the JESSI initiative exceptional R&D efforts and extremely high investment is necessary. The micro-electronics industry cannot afford these investments alone.[35]

JESSI funding on the government side comes both from national governments and from the Commission. As an evolution of the ESPRIT model, this extended span of funding coordination and sector scope is an important new feature.

In May 1989, the European Information Technology Industry Roundtable released a *White Paper on European I.T.* (Information Technology) *Industry and the Single Market*. It spells out some general objectives for the next phase of policy development. The most significant are these:

- To widen and elevate the channel of communication by establishing a formal procedure based on periodic meetings between all the commissioners, including the president, and the chief executives of the twelve major European companies.

- To extend the range of consultation beyond R&D to cover external trade, a number of internal market regulations, such as government procurement and standards, and competition policy.

The *White Paper* notes:

> Up to now, R&D initiatives of the Commission . . . have created confidence and strengthened European cooperation within the [information technology] industry. [But] concentrating on R&D cooperation is no longer sufficient. . . . The next step should be to set a goal-oriented strategy with the objective of gaining competi-

tive advantage. This requires the creation of major initiatives targeted at specific markets and technologies.[36]

In summary, as the 1990s begin, the strategic orientation and implementing elements of EC innovation policy, so far centered on information technology, have been defined in a more coherent fashion than is evident in the United States. The overall objective of the policy is to restore and enhance European competitiveness vis-à-vis Japan and the United States. The policy instruments are technology, trade, and market structure (competition policy). This is the mandate provided the Commission in the Single European Act and endorsed by the key players in European industry. In information technology, the Japanese model of close and continuing government-industry cooperation has been a major influence. Both the trade and the competition elements remain to be fully enunciated, as do, *a fortiori*, the specifics of coordination among the three instruments.

CONCLUSIONS

A number of long-term, underlying trends coincided in the 1980s to create a mounting interest in the broad issue of technology/competitiveness in the Triad. This is spurring a move to a new policy set—innovation policy. Although trade policy is an element in the set, domestic policies—regulatory and R&D—are also key, as is the interaction among them. These developments are having and will increasingly have international implications. One of these implications is already clear: a move in one bloc of the Triad evokes a countermove in the others. This "policy spillover" means, inter alia, that the unintended consequences of any action risk outweighing the explicit objectives. The spillover effect is observable at both the governmental and the firm level. Global corporations have played a major, albeit different, role in the policy evolution in each bloc of the Triad.

The emergence of innovation policy underlines another trend in the world economic system: the blurring of the boundary between domestic and international policy. The Uruguay Round, of course, as already noted, has exposed such a trend; indeed, the divisiveness it has provoked over many issues has provided vociferous testimony to this fact.

A good example concerns investment. The Uruguay Round, if successful, will treat a limited number of "trade-related" measures, because of opposition to the very notion of the GATT's treating investment at all (investment, the argument goes, is a domestic matter related to growth and development). That this approach will be inadequate to deal with international friction in this area is quite clear from what is happening in the international economy. Since the early 1980s OECD foreign direct investment flows have tripled, vastly outstripping trade growth of less than 5 percent a year, and this is a trend likely to accelerate. (Japanese direct investment outflows, which have been very modest in the past, accelerated from $7 billion in 1985 to more than $34 billion in 1988, and to an annual rate of $41 billion in the first three quarters of 1989.[37]) The sharp rise in foreign demand for U.S. real assets in the late 1980s, which is one of the reasons for the prolonged "sustainability" of the current account deficit, has already produced political pressure to control foreign takeovers.[38]

Innovation policy takes this process of blurring the distinction between international and domestic policies much further. True, innovation policy contains a trade element. This is clear from at least the early period in Japan and also is becoming evident in both the United States and the EC, though in somewhat different ways, in antidumping. But in addition to trade and R&D policy, a third element is related to market structure, where competition policy and aspects of financial market regulation are relevant. The direct and indirect *trade* consequences of such a policy set are hardly obvious—indeed, to provide acceptable empirical quantification would be extremely difficult. Again, the contrast with the agenda of the Uruguay Round yields insights. In the case of agriculture, it took 40 years to get agreement on the basic idea that the cause of the trade problem was domestic intervention. The OECD measurement of the producer subsidy equivalent, by bringing to light in a summary index number the "quantum" of intervention in each country, played a crucial role in forcing the debate, at OECD ministerial meetings and summits, a debate which finally got agriculture on the Uruguay Round agenda. This, again, serves to underline the point that in innovation policy, which undoubtedly has and will likely continue to have important international consequences, we are dealing with an issue that is of a quantum difference in order of magnitude from those international/domestic policies now on the table in Geneva. The GATT was designed to deal with a simpler world, in which international trade issues were centered primarily on border measures mainly in the form of tariffs.

One final point deserves mention as an illustration of blurring boundaries and international friction. Shortly after the United States named Japan under the super 301 provision of the Omnibus Trade Act, the Structural Impediments Initiative (SII) was established to identify and deal with "structural problems in both countries that impede trade and to improve international payments imbalances."[39] The U.S. list includes land use, savings, distribution, exclusionary business practices, and retail pricing. The Japanese list covers savings, corporate investment, corporate culture, government regulations (including export controls, domestic preference, and antitrust law), R&D, and manpower education and training. Blurring boundaries indeed! The lists include everything from macro policy and regulation to consumer tastes and producer preferences. Thus, it should be noted, a serious danger lies in the notion of "blurring boundaries": if it is argued that virtually everything affects "competitiveness," the only practicable solution will be managed trade.

This view is expressed most forcefully as follows:

> The path down which the United States is currently going in its negotiations with Japan under the rubric of Structural Impediments Initiative . . . , where matters such as Japan's retail distribution system and even her "high" savings rate are being discussed as obstacles to trade, is the path of folly. This is so, not merely because it proceeds on a one-on-one basis without the benefit of general procedures uniformly applying to all. It is also because, once one starts bringing into the trade arena issues such as even savings rates, one is essentially arguing that everything affects trade, that policy (or absence thereof) on virtually everything will affect trade, and therefore every policy can be put on the line in discussing what is "fair trade" and hence a prerequisite for legitimate free trade. . . . In going down this unwise trade route, the American trade policymakers put the world trading system at great risk. For, if *everything* becomes a question of fair trade, the only outcome will be to remove altogether the possibility of ever agreeing to a rule-

oriented trading system. "Managed trade" will then be the outcome, with bureaucrats allocating trade according to what domestic lobbying pressures and foreign political muscle dictate.[40]

With this danger clearly in mind, we turn in chapter 4 to policy recommendations.

4

CONCLUSIONS

The Uruguay Round is extraordinarily ambitious and even if moderately successful will result in a significant extension and reinforcement of the liberal, multilateral trading system. However, as this study has attempted to demonstrate, since its launch in September 1986, a number of developments in the international economy and in policy point to emerging new trade-related issues that are not on the table in Geneva. The seeds from which these issues sprouted were planted long before 1986, of course, but when the policy process of governments is confronted by rapid change, the lag in response tends to produce systemic myopia.

The developments tracked in the analysis essentially boil down to three:

- A decline in priority of the broad foreign policy "milieu goals" that have governed U.S. trade policy in the postwar period.

- An increasing focus in both the EC and the United States on the importance of a domestic base in "strategic sectors" (in the externalities or security sense), especially information technology, as a key to competitiveness in international trade.

- An erosion of the liberal, multilateral trade policy consensus paradigm in the discipline of economics.

These three developments are obviously interrelated, but it is not the purpose of this study to explore their links. It is important to note, however, that information technology—or, more precisely, information and communication technology—is not simply a cluster of innovations but rather what has been termed a new technoeconomic paradigm, which (as steam power did in the mid-nineteenth century) is affecting all sectors of industry and the organization and structure of firms. The information and communication technology revolution has provided, as well, the *means* for globalization of *industry*. One expert has also argued that elements of Japanese innovation policy were particularly well suited to early identification and exploitation of information and communication technology.[1] (This serendipity appears to be less clear in the case of software or the biotechnology cluster of innovations which may generate fundamental and pervasive change in the next century.)

While public policy systems are inherently myopic and inertial, they do respond, after a long lag, to accumulating changes in public opinion that then build up sufficient strength to overcome the dominant view. It is only at such times that a fundamental change in the trend of policy is possible.[2] The argument presented in this study is *not* that such a fundamental change *has occurred*, but that the "cross-currents" (to use Dicey's term) in opinion in opposition to the dominant postwar multilateral orientation are becoming stronger. No alternate systemic view has yet emerged from these cross-currents, but if and when it does, it may well become sufficiently strong to replace the dominant view. In the meantime, the transition is likely to be untidy or even turbulent unless policy initiatives are undertaken to adapt the postwar model, in an incremental fashion, to the new international economy.

The GATT was designed to deal primarily with border protection in the form of tariffs, and it did so with enormous success. Confronted in the 1970s with the rise of nontariff barriers, both domestic and border, the Tokyo Round of the 1970s was less successful. Some of the unfinished business of that round, as well as the extension of the GATT model to services and other new issues, is the task of the Uruguay Round. But an emergent third form of protection—offensive rather than defensive—essentially lies outside the Uruguay Round or, indeed, the orientation of the GATT. One can also see signs of a fourth wave, which has already received the title of "green protectionism" (the U.S.–EC beef hormone dispute and the Chilean grape debacle are just the beginning), as the political cross-currents of the environmental movement gather steam.[3] Indeed, the best way to track such cross-currents in an age of information and communication technology is through the popular media: *Time* magazine named the "endangered earth" its man of the year in January 1989!

Another significant trend that began in the 1980s has been the move, first among industrialized countries but spilling over recently to many other parts of the world, to convergence in a range of domestic regulatory and other micro policy areas. As I noted earlier, this process has come under the general umbrella of structural adjustment, and the G-7 and the OECD have initiated increasingly formalized multilateral surveillance procedures. In some respects the U.S.–Japanese Structural Impediments Initiative (SII) is part of the same process, except that it is oriented to market access, and some policy convergence is seen only as a means to that end. Moreover, as already noted, the SII shopping lists cover such a mélange of policies, preferences, behavioral patterns, and so forth that it heightens the risk of a move to bilateral managed trade.

The pressure for policy convergence emanates from the increasing interdependence of the international economy and the information and communication technology revolution. The most advanced model of convergence now on the horizon is that emerging in Europe from the move to complete the internal market, or Europe 1992. This is worth spelling out.

The choice laid out in the 1985 Commission *White Paper* to base the market completion on "mutual recognition" rather than on prior harmonization of government regulations in effect launched a process described by one analyst as follows:

> competition between different regulatory systems ... which is exactly the same as the competition among suppliers of goods.... [This] free competition among different locations and hence among the tax and expenditure systems and the rules and regulations prevailing there ... is government competition for internationally mobile resources, such as capital and entrepreneurship and also labour with a high content of human capital.[4]

This process of competition will produce convergence (harmonization) at the level of intervention that best reflects the preferences of the mobile resources, especially capital and entrepreneurship.

For the EC two conditions are essential for this more advanced (that is, than peer group pressure through multilateral surveillance) process of convergence: mutual recognition and mobility of the key factors of production. Neither of these conditions exists globally, nor does any multilateral institution at the present time have a mandate to initiate their implementation. Moreover, the differences in government regulation are far greater within the Triad than among the member-states of the EC. In addition, concerns about competitiveness in the United States go beyond the economic into security considerations in some instances. Finally, there are not yet any truly "global" multinationals—that is, without national identity—in the sense that Europe 1992 is creating truly "European" corporations. There are, rather, Japanese, American, German, and so forth, multinationals in a process of global adaptation. Governments are concerned about the competitiveness of their economies and of their corporations, and, to a large degree, they still equate the two.

Yet the heart of the innovation policy debate—Japanese targeting and all that—relates to the idea of governmental or locational competition. If, as has been argued here and elsewhere, in technologically sophisticated industries "market organization" in its broadest sense affects firms' performance and this market organization is itself affected by government policy, then ideally what would be needed for convergence would be competition among innovation policy paradigms, rather than only among the goods and services that are partly proxies for such paradigms. In such a system, the mobile factors of production would determine the "optimum" policy paradigm, and consumer preferences (which must be accepted as given) would determine which products were competitive.

It is important to stress the distinction between consumer tastes and the capability of individual enterprises on the one hand, and government micro policy on the other. In this context it is useful to spell out more fully that one of the more serious risks in the U.S. bilateral approach is that it has elicited from a number of quarters the Japanese-are-so-different-that-special-rules-are-required-only-for-them view. Underlying this view is the notion of profound, immutable cultural differences, and adherents to this perspective provide many examples of consumer and producer behavior to buttress their proposition. The conclusion is quite clear. Either the Japanese have to behave "just like us" (which is impossible) or the special rules needed are managed trade based on results.

The idea of policy convergence is quite different. It accepts as given different tastes and preferences (French and German consumers are certainly not identical) and differing performance capabilities of individual enterprises, but also accepts that government policies affect the performance of market participants. It is these policies that need to be harmonized, and as the EC hopes, the process of *optimal* harmonization can best be achieved by competition. *The object is not to harmonize tastes, culture, and corporate behavior, but to optimize factor mobility and competition.*

Since such an approach is out of reach for the foreseeable future (and, indeed, its success is not entirely assured even in Europe, where some degree of reregulation at the Community level is also foreseen), the recommendations that follow are pragmatic, second-best (or tenth-best!) alternatives to achieve a greater measure of convergence in key policies. They relate to policy proposals in the OECD and the GATT, and, finally, to the role of the global corporation.

THE OECD: INNOVATION POLICY

Because the innovation policy set embraces such a range of government programs, the OECD, which has expertise in all the different areas, is the logical locus for initiating a project for analysis and policy proposals. (If it were possible to include some of the NIEs in the exercise, although they are not OECD members, that would greatly add to the value of the convergence mechanism.)

The objectives of the initiative would be to do the following:

- Review the theoretical and empirical literature on "strategic industries" with a view to proposing a *consensus working definition* for policy use.

- Analyze the three elements of the policy set—trade, R&D, and market structure policies—in (initially) the Triad, with a view to highlighting the *impact* of significant differences in policy *on industrial and trade performance.*

- Make recommendations for *short-run* action (to defuse international friction) and to implement a *longer-run process of policy convergence.*

The key question that impels the proposal is: How much divergence in policy systems can an ever-more interdependent international economy sustain? The first objective (defining strategic industries in the externalities/security sense) requires little elaboration. The literature on technological change, trade and industrial policy, and so forth is large and growing. The analytic review should focus on the definitional elements and on the empirical evidence on externalities, security, and so on. This task is likely to be a continuing one, and it would be an essential part of the exercise to publish results so that not only governments but also key industrial and consumer participants in the policy-making process are kept abreast of the analysis.

The notion of "strategic industries" at present provides a wide-open door to pleas for intervention. Subjecting the concept to analytic and empirical investigation might not close the door but would certainly leave it only partly ajar. Further, if governments could agree on a consensus working definition, it should be possible to monitor subsidies and other types of special treatment (for example, taxes) for these sectors on a continuing basis. A consultative forum, to handle policy disputes in these sectors, would also be useful.

The second objective (the comparative analysis of the policy set) is far more complex and will require consultation among experts to flesh out fully. The difficulty arises mainly not in the trade or R&D field but in the combination of policies that directly or indirectly affect market structure and influence corporate performance.

One obvious candidate in this element is competition policy. Marked differences are apparent within the Triad not only in the law but, more important, in the application of the law. This is an

CONCLUSIONS □ 85

opportune time to launch such an analysis, because the European Commission's role in mergers policy is evolving under the 1992 mandate, and also because, as we have seen, a process of reform may well begin in the United States. Further, a good deal of what is regarded as "unique" in Japan—the distribution system, or aspects of the *keiretsu*, for example—is related to the manner in which Japanese competition policy is administered.[5] Thus it would be important not simply to compare what is "on the books" but the application and enforcement of the policy and the impact of the enforcement (or nonenforcement) on company behavior, a much more complex task.

But competition policy is not the whole story. A major determinant of competitiveness is investment. And differences in the cost of capital among countries are very important in influencing investment performance. While many factors affect the cost of capital—including macro policy, household savings behavior, and tax policy—differences in capital market structure also account for significant differences in capital cost among countries in the Triad regions.[6]

One key difference relates to the role of banks, which is much greater with respect to corporate financing in Japan and Germany than in North America and the United Kingdom. (This also affects foreign takeover activity, as noted below.) A Federal Reserve Bank of New York study points out the following:

> Close relations between corporations and banks in Japan and Germany and official efforts in these countries to reduce the private costs of corporate distress permit corporations to finance themselves in ways that cheapen the costs of funds. In particular, greater integration of industry and banking in Japan and Germany has permitted higher leveraging without raising bankruptcy rates much above those in the United States and Britain. The stronger ties between corporate borrowers and their banks also reduce the liquidity risk that a firm runs by borrowing so much at short term. Backstopping private creditors' management of difficulties is the Japanese and German governments' predictable willingness to spread the adjustment costs beyond the immediately involved workers, management, creditors and shareholders to business customers, consumers and taxpayers.[7]

Of course, during the 1980s the growth of equity markets and foreign investment in equities brought some change in this bank-dominated model. In Japan,

> slower growth of the Japanese economy ... and the growing access of larger Japanese corporations to bond finance and, through equity warrant, to equity finance in the Euromarket are freeing them from reliance on their traditional banks to finance growth. ... The equity crossholdings between Japanese banks and their borrowers may diminish ... as Japanese banks attempt to meet the new international capital standards. Japanese banks are looking to raise sums of equity through issuance of shares, convertible bonds, and equity warrants in Tokyo and London: their traditional shareholders may well wind up with a relatively diminished stake.[8]

The controversy over bank power has stirred a vigorous debate in Germany. Moreover, the U.S. financial markets will undergo further restructuring that is likely to involve some integration of banking, securities, and insurance activities.

But the differences will remain significant. In the case of Germany, the changes in capital market arrangements and industrial policy will evolve under the momentum generated by Europe 1992 and the process of convergence described above.[9] In Japan the nexus of relationship between capital markets and industrial structure (the *keiretsu*) is both far more complex and far more pervasive in its impact not only on capital cost but on risk sharing, and thus on the quality as well as on the quantity of investment. The only impetus to greater convergence in these policies between Japan and other countries at the present time is American pressure through the Structural Impediments Initiative. It bears repeating that the danger of this bilateral approach is that it risks being converted to a targeted results-oriented managed trade arrangement. Instead of dealing with the underlying market structure issues, this would, in fact, force the Japanese to engage in further government intervention in shaping corporate behavior—in other words, it would result not in greater *convergence* but in greater *divergence* than now exists. While the OECD alternative will not provide a quicker fix—because one does not exist—it has the merit of trying to direct attention to basic causes and not to symptoms.[10] It would, however, be counterproductive if it were seen to be a means of avoiding or delaying rather than facilitating policy convergence.

In trade policy, a comparative analysis of barriers would be useful, but is unlikely to add much to what is already known—that is, that within the Triad, tariff and nontariff measures exhibit no significant measurable differences. The Uruguay Round should, if possible, deal with antidumping policy reform (see below), although published OECD proposals in this regard would be helpful. Intellectual property is another key area in innovation policy where the aim of the Uruguay Round is, in fact, to achieve greater policy convergence, not only in the OECD, where the differences in standards of protection are not very great, but between the OECD and the developing countries, where norms and standards show wide divergence in levels of protection. But perhaps the most important issue to highlight at the present time would be the R&D subsidy area. A broad treatment of this, covering not only direct government defense and nondefense expenditure, but also tax expenditure items, might serve as input into a revised subsidy code (perhaps confined at first to specific sectors, as suggested above) in the Uruguay Round.

If we include investment along with trade policy, it would be important for the OECD analysis to go beyond the Uruguay Round agenda item of trade-related investment measures. What is required is a comparative analysis of foreign direct investment flows and of the differences among the Triad in de jure and de facto impediments to access. As I have already noted, the change in the composition of the capital flows financing the external deficit of the United States in the direction of foreign direct investment and takeover activity[11] has already begun to generate friction. This friction will be greatly exacerbated if significant asymmetry of access prevails within the Triad. Such friction is already apparent in the marked differences in the rules governing takeovers as between Japan and the United States (and, indeed, has led to some changes in those rules), but differences in capital market structure (the extensive interlocking group shareholding of companies and banks) also impede takeovers in Japan. A major impediment to foreign takeovers, of course, is the very high price/earnings ratios in the Japanese equity market. But greater access to that market by foreign firms would help reduce the differences in capital cost.[12]

Finally, in R&D policy, as we have seen, convergence seems to be occurring on the Japanese-inspired precompetitive research consortium. At the present time these consortia exclude foreign subsidiaries, and one obvious area for early policy reform would be to develop codes governing conditions of access, on a reciprocal basis, to government-financed consortia.

But this issue of emergent protectionism in the R&D area will require more intensive analysis and more far-ranging policy proposals. The policy predisposition to contain the diffusion of technological knowledge within national boundaries runs counter to a powerful globalizing trend in R&D both by corporations and by research institutions and universities. The internationalization of research is also fed by emerging global markets for research personnel who can produce and apply it. An attempt to "nationalize" technology in the face of such powerful trends is unlikely to be successful and can be very deleterious by fostering duplication of effort and thus lowering the private rate of return to technological change, reducing the accessibility to scientific knowledge, and diminishing the potential benefits to world growth. For this reason, what are required are not only policy proposals to deal with the current issue of access but a more thorough review of policy options for mutually beneficial international cooperation appropriate to a new era of "borderless technology."

The foregoing has set out some examples of the analytic and policy questions that would form the basis of an OECD initiative on the innovation policy issue. But the crucial element in the proposal is how to implement an ongoing process to achieve policy convergence. The analysis is a means to that end. While some short-term policy action may be feasible, in either the OECD or the Uruguay Round, achieving harmonization of policy will be a much more difficult process.

The multilateral surveillance approach in the OECD and the G-7 relies essentially on transparency (analysis and exchange of information) and peer group pressure. These are, indeed, the sole instruments of international policy coordination (or of regulatory harmonization, as in the case of banking under the Cooke committee of the Bank for International Settlements) in the absence of a rules-based regime. They are, for example, the only basis for international macroeconomic policy coordination since the breakdown of the Bretton Woods system of fixed exchange rates. The process of multilateral surveillance of macro policy has, since the Tokyo Summit in 1986, become increasingly formalized in the forum of the G-7 finance ministers and officials. The IMF has assumed a secretariat function, providing information and analysis to facilitate discussion and enhance the peer process of fostering domestic policies that are compatible with international stability and sustainable growth.

What I have argued here is that the rules-based GATT regime is not appropriate to deal with the innovation policy set. In certain elements—antidumping, subsidies, and intellectual property are examples—convergence can be instituted in a reformed and strengthened GATT. And over time, the new trade policy review mechanism, which is part of the Uruguay Round agenda, may be sufficiently strengthened and extended to deal with some of the issues. One can even envisage that over the longer run, a set of GATT codes might be developed for some policies. But for the present, the process of surveillance to promote a consensus on policy harmonization lies well beyond the capacity and the mandate of the GATT.

The approach suggested here would be to produce from the OECD analysis the more significant elements of divergence in the innovation policy set and highlight the impact of this divergence on industrial and trade performance. This analysis would provide the framework for the policy discussion (just as the analysis of the current account imbalances provided the overall framework or focus for the multilateral surveillance of macro policy in the latter half of the 1980s). The objective of the OECD process would be to draw up a mutually agreed set of *policy guidelines*, a *timetable for reform*, and a *means of monitoring progress* through, perhaps, the development of quantitative indicators.

These are extremely complex issues and would require skilled secretariat assistance in providing objective analysis and information. This is good reason to launch the process as quickly as possible, perhaps with the assistance of outside experts and business representatives in the analytic phase of the initiative and, as mentioned, reaching out beyond the present OECD membership if feasible. The output of this analysis would then be fed into a special committee. Because the subject matter covers a number of areas, the committee's effective operation would require a greater degree of coordination within national capitals than is customary. (In this sense, it is a more difficult exercise than the G-7 multilateral surveillance, which focuses primarily on monetary and fiscal policy. The policy convergence process is thus more akin to the OECD structural adjustment activity.) But greater coordination within national capitals is, of course, desirable in and of itself, however difficult to launch and maintain.

Finally, it is important to underline again that while policy convergence is desirable, it will not miraculously dissolve all points of international friction. Differences in consumer tastes and preferences will remain. Rules matter to corporations, of course, but corporate players have different styles, statures, and capacities. Market structures can only set the *parameters* within which corporations *operate*. A firm's behavior also reflects its corporate strategy and national infrastructure, such as the educational system and, of course, the macro environment. In the last analysis, it will be corporate performance that really matters.

So the convergence exercise must be distinguished from the much-touted notion of a level playing field. That metaphor is vague enough to include everything.[13] The level playing field concept has to be narrowed to embrace legitimate and practicable objectives that are best approximated by policy convergence—that is, playing by the *same rules*. The alternative is to specify the score in advance of the game.

THE GATT: ANTIDUMPING AND SAFEGUARDS

As we saw in the account on antidumping in the previous chapter, a number of significant, essentially unilateral, changes in regulation have occurred in the past few years—after the launch of the Uruguay Round. In September 1986, the reform of antidumping was not a priority for any contracting party. More recently, however, because of concern about the developments described, a number of countries have submitted proposals for reform of various aspects of the Tokyo code (including consideration of rules of origin for the first time in the GATT).

However, it is certainly not clear at this stage what changes will be adopted. As we have seen, in the United States, and to a lesser extent in Europe, private-sector opposition to the current regulations and procedures has emerged. However, both the business community and governments are exerting strong counterpressure not only to resist significant change but to tighten procedures to make antidumping more responsive to industry demand for protection against "unfair" trade.

Logically, the principle of national treatment under domestic competition policy should replace antidumping regulation. The same definition of undesirable pricing behavior that is applied to domestic firms should apply to foreign firms exporting into the domestic market. Such logic is unlikely to prevail in this millennium, however. The arguments against this neat solution are twofold.

The first relates to the idea of strategic sectors described above. In this context dumping is seen as a new form of firms' predatory pricing to secure market share in such sectors. The argument, then, is that dumping must be controlled in order to ensure a domestic base in these sectors because of either "rents" or externalities. Of course, it would, in theory, be possible to deal with this issue as a special exemption from the national treatment procedure.

The second argument against the competition policy approach is more compelling and relates to our previous discussion of convergence. Because competition policy differs significantly among countries (in this instance, with respect to the treatment of pricing behavior), the application of a national treatment principle would result in substantial divergence in international pricing practices, which would likely be unacceptable to both many firms and countries. If, however, the OECD initiative did, over time, promote convergence in this key policy area, it should be possible to propose for consideration in the GATT at some future date this more fundamental approach to the reform of antidumping.

Within the allotted time frame of the Uruguay Round, negotiations in each group will have to be completed by mid-1990 and the entire package must be pulled together by the close of the year to meet the deadline at the end of 1990. So, at best, it is likely that only modest changes are feasible.

Clearly, the present GATT antidumping code is too vague and is, because of changes in the international economy, incomplete. Contracting parties thus have been able to implement unilateral interpretations and claim GATT-consistency. Many of these interpretations go in the direction of facilitating the finding of dumping and of expanding antidumping measures. Some also have involved the use of one policy instrument, a mechanism intended to deal with a specific unfair trade practice, to achieve other policy objectives quite unrelated to dumping per se. Thus the overall objective of the Uruguay Round reform should be to constrain these unilateral interpretations by extending or clarifying and making more specific those aspects of the code that have allowed this proliferation.

These aspects are both *procedural* and *substantive*. A full and detailed set of proposals in this regard is beyond the scope of this presentation.[14] But the analysis presented in chapter 2 does provide some examples of priority candidates. On the procedural side, the GATT code requires a specific provision on circumvention, a uniform rule of origin, a provision to ensure that users are represented at hearings, and a rule governing *disclosure of information*. On the substantive side, clear and specific provisions should be added to specify *dumping determination* (that is, determination of foreign market value), export prices, adjustments to bring both to a comparable basis, and the calculation of the dumping margin. (I have not discussed other, untidy issues in injury determination.) These changes would, at least, constrain unilateralism and, through increased transparency and countervalence, help prevent any further expansion of the protectionist drift evident in the 1980s. The four big users—the United States, the EC, Canada, and Australia—are key to any reform.

Reinstating antidumping as a legitimate safety valve might also require provision for special "fast-track" and "repeat-offender" procedures to deal with specific sectors—for example, those agreed as strategic in the OECD exercise. This is clearly a difficult and contentious issue, but it may be worthwhile considering as a quid pro quo for the other reforms. Finally, a GATT surveillance and dispute settlement mechanism should be established under the code. Among the tasks assigned the surveillance body should be the regular and timely publication of statistics on antidumping.

One other condition is probably necessary (though not sufficient) for antidumping reform in this round—a new safeguard arrangement to deal with "fair" trade. Over the 1980s, antidumping became a thinly disguised selective safeguard protection against increased imports just as voluntary export restraints (VERs) and similar measures have been used in lieu of the GATT-sanctioned article 19. (The ratio of VERs to article 19 has been estimated as more than three to one since the late 1970s.)[15]

Article 19 of the GATT, honored more in the breach than in the observance, permits temporary protection measures (safeguards) when a sudden influx of imports threatens serious injury to a domestic industry. Thus far, securing agreement on reform has proved impossible since the Tokyo Round. The sticking point has been the demand by some countries, notably the EC, that selective application (that is, to particular countries) be explicitly permitted. Other countries, especially developing countries, have strongly resisted this, on the grounds that it would legalize a principle fundamentally at variance with the GATT: the MFN rule that trade measures should not discriminate among countries.

The paradox is clear. Countries have refrained from using article 19 and chosen instead selective VERs or the trade remedy laws, which, by definition, are selectively applied. These choices are also preferable because they do not require the country that invokes them to "compensate" the exporting country by liberalizing trade for products other than those subject to the safeguard action; they involve, instead, a transfer of income from consumers to the foreign producer, who holds the quota, by way of higher profits (or rents). Since consumers rarely are organized enough to complain, the politics of VERs seem attractive.

One way around this conundrum would be to include selectivity as part of a "menu of options" in a revised safeguard clause. But in order to constrain its use, different "prices" should be charged for each item on the menu. Thus, for example, if the most desirable option is protection by tariff on an MFN basis, the price for that should be very low: limited compensation combined with a gradual reduction of the tariff over a specified time period. Selective protection by quantitative restriction, preferably negotiated by the importing and exporting country, should be the most "expensive": substantial compensation and significant reduction of the quotas over a relatively short time period. Other combinations could obviously be added to the menu. A surveillance mechanism, geared to monitoring the adjustment of the protected industry and publicizing VERs negotiated outside the GATT safeguard arrangement would also be desirable. Second helpings of any item on the menu should carry a very high price tag. After all, the Multi Fibre Arrangement has gone on for over 25 years, and consumers have paid an enormous bill.

Finally, as I have repeatedly stressed throughout this study, the Uruguay Round should be regarded as a "new beginning" in strengthening multilateralism. Ideally, periodic GATT rounds should be abandoned: the world economy is changing too rapidly for this traditional approach. Continuing negotiations and an enhanced institutional capacity to monitor the international economy are necessary to prevent once again the serious erosion of credibility and relevance that took place in the 1970s and 1980s. But in practical terms, in order to mobilize political and private-sector interest and support, negotiating rounds are still necessary. Ideally, a new round should be launched as soon as the December 1990 Brussels meeting of ministers adopting the Uruguay package is over.

The main reason for this proposal is that the Uruguay Round is heavily oriented to extending rules rather than to opening markets. This is particularly true in the new issues of services and trade-related investment.

In order to rebuild the commitment of the private sector, a GATT negotiation should result in improved market access, that is, significant trade liberalization. Thus, for example, if a General Agreement on Trade in Services (GATS) could be developed by the end of 1990, that would be an enormous achievement. But it would not be enough. Sectoral negotiations (probably initially involving a group of like-minded countries on a "plurilateral" conditional MFN basis) should be commenced immediately in 1991. Similarly, in the case of investment, the Uruguay Round result is likely to be limited to a few trade-related measures. But in view of the increasing importance of investment flows in the international economy, a broader approach is essential. Once again, this might have to be launched by a group of like-minded countries. This idea of reciprocal treatment on a plurilateral basis is a realistic and necessary compromise between bilateral reciprocity and the GATT principle of unconditional MFN, which, as GATT membership has grown larger and more diverse, has made negotiations on nontraditional issues increasingly difficult and painfully slow. The resulting frustration of many businessmen has been amply documented here and elsewhere.

Of course, a new round in 1991 centered on market access could not be confined only to services and investment. For a variety of reasons, the Uruguay Round market access negotiations are unlikely to include a "big package" in the traditional areas either, so a further push in such sectors would provide a reasonable quid pro quo for the developing countries. Also, plenty of business in agriculture is likely to be left unfinished from the Uruguay Round and should be included on the agenda. And on the general issue of technology, further cooperation in the area of a strengthened subsidy code and, if required, intellectual property should be considered.

It is, however, not the purpose here to lay out a detailed agenda for a post-Uruguay GATT round. The key issue is rather how to build on the "new beginning" established by the Uruguay Round. What would be on the table in a new round, in effect, is a continuation of the long and difficult process of reestablishing the preeminence of multilateralism as the basic framework for the world trading system. If that is to be accomplished, however, it cannot be left only to government officials negotiating in Geneva. It would also require the active support of the private sector and especially the global corporation. And given the findings of this study, the prospects for fulfilling that requirement are not very bright. Let me then turn, in conclusion, to that subject.

THE GLOBAL CORPORATIONS

As has been amply demonstrated in the discussion of the political economy of policymaking, the global corporations play an important, though different, role in each bloc of the Triad. But only the American corporations are active in the high policy process of the Uruguay Round. The one exception to this has been the participation of some European and Japanese corporations in the negotiating groups specifically concerned with services and intellectual property.

During 1990 in Geneva the priorities will be first to complete negotiation in each of the fifteen negotiating groups, and then to put together the final package, which will, of course, involve horse trading among agenda items. So even for those corporations with the narrowest concerns—say, patent protection for drugs—a more broadly based orientation would be necessary to help ensure a successful outcome.

Be that as it may, the account of the political economy of policymaking in the Triad presented in this study, which contrasts, in the case of the GATT round, the pluralist activism of the United States with the neutrality or indifference of the Europeans and Japanese, raises an interesting question: Who is out of step? Perhaps, as I have suggested, the U.S. model, stemming from the unique character of the American system of governance, is sui generis. American firms have always lobbied Congress: the structure of most firms includes a lobby function. Hence, the structure of the large multinational firm in the United States today will nearly always include a unit dedicated to "government relations" or public (including international) policy. Counterparts in Europe or Japan are rare. So the observed differences are not superficial but deep-seated, both in the society and in corporate structure and strategy. Convergence of the political economy high policy paradigms would be very difficult and, in the absence of a strongly felt need, seems unlikely at present.

This leaves the multilateral policy process largely in the domain of governments, and the government-business "alliance" in the United States. As I have suggested, one should not assume that the traditional let-Uncle-Sam-do-it view is a safe bet today. Thus, if the United States can achieve most of its trade policy objectives more efficiently and effectively with a combination of section 301 investigations and bilateral free trade agreements, how long will it continue to uphold the rule of law of multilateralism rather than deploy the enormous power of its large market?[16]

In the case of innovation policy, as we have seen, center stage is dominated by the activist model of the Japanese, with its close and pervasive links between government and business. While this has set in motion some changes in Europe and the United States, at the level of both government and the government-industry interface, the outcome of that process is far from clear. Especially in the United States, deeply rooted cultural factors in the business community will militate against the establishment of a close and continuing relationship between government and the multinationals, even in strategic sectors. The differences in political economy will continue to be a source of international friction.

But if we move beyond the present divergence in the political economy of policymaking in the Triad, it is worthwhile asking whether a more fundamental trend is under way. This study has focused on only one sector of the business community—the so-called global (a much overused word, admittedly) corporation. While the terminology in the business school literature, whence the term arises, is not yet settled, as pointed out earlier, the idea of a global firm is one operating on a world scale and on the basis of a worldwide, rather than multicountry, strategy. Few firms are truly global, but many are globalizing through a new wave of investment and strategic alliances. Perhaps in the future, not only will truly global firms be exchange rate-neutral, as the Japanese seem to be becoming, but because the options of trade or investment or both are open, they will become neutral or indifferent about trade rules, as well, in the belief that they can adapt to any "rules" governments establish. We have seen an example of such adaptation in the Japanese investment response to European antidumping and perceived domestic context. (The Japanese and Koreans still have a long way to go, however, to match the Americans, who had a head start after the war. American-owned multinationals produce about $500 billion within the EC while U.S.–based producers export about $70 billion.[17])

But this neutrality strategy has several problems. First, it will lead to a growing division within the business community between the "haves," the global corporations, and the "have-nots," the firms that are less mobile and more trade-dependent (import or export). Second, governments will not easily accept the denationalization of enterprise and will, in the nature of the political process, likely be more alert to the views of the less-mobile firms and to the immobile factors generally—that is, most of the labor force. (Indeed, this is already apparent in the U.S. Congress.[18]) Third, as I stressed at the outset, the indirect consequences of any specific decision may well outweigh the stated objective. In the case of antidumping, or assumptions about regional blocs, the investment consequences may be creating problems of future overcapacity in particular sectors or, as we have seen in the case of antidumping, of competitiveness for user industries of intermediate products. Finally, while adaptation may be a feasible option for a global corporation—albeit perhaps at some cost—the absence of multilateral rules is bound to increase uncertainty. As I have emphasized, a *distorted* but *stable* system (with respect to either exchange rates or trade rules) may be acceptable to a global corporation. But an *uncertain* and *unstable* system seems bound to affect long-range planning in a deleterious fashion.

So I return to my point of departure. The international public good of a multilateral trading system is stability, the reduction of uncertainty. The erosion of the GATT has, in truth, reduced even this fundamental aspect of the system as the rules have become less and less relevant to the reality of international interdependence. The only way of restoring the true "international public good" is to restore, update, and strengthen the system. The global corporations ultimately have a large stake in this: it is the reduction of uncertainty. The fact that many do not now feel it in their interest to play a more active part in the strengthening and extension of multilateralism at a crucial period of transition to a multipolar world stems from myopia, not global vision. A far better option to serve their long-run interests would be the establishment of a global business roundtable to work with governments and the GATT for a new round in 1991.

NOTES

1. INTRODUCTION

1. See, for example, Christopher A. Bartlett and Sumantra Ghoshal, *Managing across Borders: The Transnational Solution* (Boston: Harvard Business School Press, 1989), for discussion of various concepts of the multinational. The authors prefer the term "transnational" to "global."
2. See, for example, Helen V. Milner, *Resisting Protectionism: Global Industries and the Politics of International Trade* (Princeton, N.J.: Princeton University Press, 1988), for a comparison of France and the United States in selected industries. An international comparative analysis of corporate response to the upheaval in the petrochemical industry based on intensive interviews at both management and government levels is presented in J. L. Bower, *When Markets Quake* (Boston: Harvard Business School Press, 1986).
3. Allan H. Meltzer, *Keynes's Monetary Theory: A Different Interpretation* (Cambridge, Mass.: Cambridge University Press, 1988).
4. See Jagdish Bhagwati, *Protectionism* (Cambridge, Mass.: MIT Press, 1988), pp. 54–59, on the ineffectiveness of the "new protectionism" in blocking trade.
5. OECD, *Economic Outlook* (Paris, June 1989), p. x.
6. Ibid., p. xi.
7. Bank for International Settlements, *59th Annual Report* (Basel, Switzerland, 1989), p. 7.
8. Charles L. Schultze, "Of Wolves, Termites, and Pussycats," *Brookings Review* (Summer 1989), p. 26.
9. "America's Wasting Disease," *Economist*, March 25, 1989, p. 71.
10. See Federal Reserve Board of New York, *Annual Report 1988* (New York, 1988), especially pp. 32–38. The inflow of foreign savings has been inadequate to compensate for the decline in capital per worker since 1982. See also Jagdish Bhagwati, "U.S. Trade Policy Today" (Paper presented at Columbia University Conference on Trade Policy, September 8, 1989). The author links the slow adjustment of the Japanese trade surplus after the dramatic rise of the yen to the voluntary export restraints (VERs) on many Japanese products. The scarcity premium these VERs generated served to cushion the impact of the appreciation and delay the price response on the part of Japanese firms.
11. William R. Cline, "Reciprocity: A New Approach to World Trade Policy," in William R. Cline, ed., *Trade Policy in the 1980's* (Washington, D.C.: Institute for International Economics, 1983), p. 125.

12. Paul K. Krugman and Richard E. Baldwin, "The Persistence of the U.S. Trade Deficit," Brookings Papers on Economic Activity, no. 1 (Washington, D.C., 1987), pp. 1–43.
13. David D. Hale, "The Dollar Outlook" (New York: Group of Thirty, 1989), p. 10.
14. For a review of this development, see C. Michael Aho and Sylvia Ostry, "Regional Trading Blocs: Pragmatic or Problematic Policy?" in William Brock and Robert Hormats, eds., *The Global Economy: America's Role in the Decade Ahead* (New York: American Assembly, 1990); and Jeffrey J. Schott, ed., *Free Trade Areas and U.S. Policy* (Washington, D.C.: Institute for International Economics, 1989).
15. Raymond Vernon, *Sovereignty at Bay: The Multinational Spread of U.S. Enterprises* (New York: Basic Books, 1971), p. 71.

2. TRADE POLICY

1. Richard N. Cooper, "Trade Policy Is Foreign Policy," *Foreign Policy* 9 (Winter 1972–73), pp. 18–36.
2. See, for example, Bhagwati, *Protectionism*, especially ch. 4; I. M. Destler and John S. Odell, *Anti-Protection: Changing Forces in United States Trade Politics* (Washington, D.C.: Institute for International Economics, 1987); and Milner, *Resisting Protectionism*.
3. As quoted in Raymond Vernon, "International Trade Policy in the 1980's," *International Studies Quarterly* (December 1982), p. 485.
4. Ibid., p. 486.
5. I. M. Destler, *American Trade Politics: System under Stress* (Washington, D.C.: Institute for International Economics and the Twentieth Century Fund, 1986), p. 3.
6. Alan William Wolff, "International Competitiveness of American Industry: The Role of U.S. Trade Policy," in Bruce R. Scott and George C. Lodge, eds., *U.S. Competitiveness in the World Economy* (Boston: Harvard Business School Press, 1985), pp. 320–321.
7. Edmund Pratt, "Intellectual Property and United States Trade Policy" (Speech before the Intellectual Property Rights Conference, Conference Board, New York, October 3, 1989), pp. 13–18. In the services sector U.S. activism has not been confined to the Triad: coalitions from nine countries now meet regularly with the GATT secretariat. A recent report of the U.S. Coalition on Developing Countries is based on its own survey. For a history of U.S. activism, see Geza Feketekuty, *International Trade in Services: An Overview and Blueprint for Negotiations* (Cambridge, Mass.: Ballinger, 1988), pp. 295–322.
8. For an assessment, see Gilbert R. Winham, *International Trade and the Tokyo Round Negotiation* (Princeton, N.J.: Princeton University Press, 1986). As Winham reports, one government official described the process of co-option thus: "When you let a dog piss all over a fire hydrant, he thinks he owns it" (p. 316). The USTR took the hydrant to the dog.
9. Destler, *American Trade Politics*, p. 94.

10. See, for example, Helen V. Milner and David B. Yoffie, "Between Free Trade and Protectionism: Strategic Trade Policy and a Theory of Corporate Trade Demands," *International Organization* (Spring 1989), pp. 239–272; and Bhagwati, "U.S. Trade Policy Today."
11. William Diebold, "Political Implications of U.S.-E.C. Economic Conflicts (III): American Trade Policy and Western Europe," *Government and Opposition: A Journal of Comparative Politics* (Summer 1987), p. 286.
12. Richard N. Cooper, "Trade Policy as Foreign Policy," in Robert M. Stern, ed., *U.S. Trade Policies in a Changing World Economy* (Cambridge, Mass.: MIT Press, 1987), p. 301.
13. Stephen D. Krasner, "Comment on Trade Policy as Foreign Policy," in Stern, *U.S. Trade Policies*, p. 300.
14. Advisory Committee for Trade Negotiations, "Chairman's Report on a New Round of Multilateral Trade Negotiations" (Submitted to the United States Trade Representative, May 15, 1985), p. 3.
15. Ibid., p. 5.
16. "Transcript of Speech to Business and Government Leaders," *The New York Times*, September 24, 1985, p. D26.
17. *Annual Report of the President of the United States on the Trade Agreements Program 1984–85* (Washington, D.C.), appendix B, pp. 114–15.
18. Judith Bello, "Section 301 of the U.S. Trade Laws: Champion of Market Liberalization" (Paper presented at the conference on The New Trends in EC and U.S. Trade Laws, College of Bruges, Annual Conference, September 1989), p. 9.
19. Advisory Committee for Trade Policy and Negotiations, *Analysis of the U.S.-Japan Trade Problem* (Washington, D.C., 1989).
20. Emergency Committee for American Trade (ECAT), *1989 Issues Paper* (Washington, D.C., 1989), p. 22.
21. Rudiger Dornbusch, Paul Krugman, and Yung Chul Park, "Meeting World Challenges: U.S. Manufacturing in the 1990's" (Rochester, N.Y.: Eastman Kodak, 1989), p. 1. For a fuller exposition of how targeting and retaliation against Japan could be implemented by the United States and, preferably, in cooperation with the EC, see Rudiger Dornbusch, "Is There a Case for Aggressive Bilateralism and How Best to Practice It?" (Paper prepared for the Brookings Institution Conference on Alternative Trade Strategies for the United States, Washington, D.C., September 12, 1989), pp. 15–16.
22. Winham, *International Trade and the Tokyo Round Negotiation*, pp. 306–344.
23. *Financial Times*, March 14, 1989, p. 21.
24. "1992 under Construction," *Economist*, July 8, 1989, p. 23.
25. Martin Wolf, "1992 Global Implications of the European Community's Programme for Completing the Internal Market," Lehrman Institute Policy Paper, series on the United States in the global economy, no. 1 (New York, 1989), pp. 27–28. See also Gardner Patterson, "The European Community as a Threat to the System," in Cline, ed., *Trade Policy in the 1980's*, pp. 223–242.
26. The more traditional view of the Commission is well expressed by Sir Roy Denman, who played a key role in the Tokyo Round. In a letter to the

author (April 18, 1989) Sir Roy pointed out that "transferring to a system of public consultation ... would ... run the risk of complicating an already delicate balance between the Commission and the member states in the decision-making process."

27. Bunroku Yoshino, "Japan and the Uruguay Round," in Henry R. Nau, ed., *Domestic Trade Politics and the Uruguay Round* (New York: Columbia University Press, 1989), pp. 111–134.
28. See, for example, Richard Samuels, *The Business of the Japanese State* (Ithaca, N.Y.: Cornell University Press, 1987), especially pp. 258–263, for a review of competing views.
29. Bower, *When Markets Quake*, pp. 220–221.
30. Stephen D. Krasner, "Trade Conflicts and the Common Defense," *Political Science Quarterly*, no. 5 (1986), pp. 794–795.
31. C. Michael Aho, "Looking at the Options," *Journal of Japanese Trade and Industry*, no. 4 (1988), pp. 14–16.
32. A potentially explosive example of this tendency to "leave it all to the Uruguay Round" concerns the acceptance, after a long delay, of a GATT panel finding that ruled that section 337 of the U.S. 1974 Trade Act did not accord with the GATT principle of "national treatment." The ruling relates to enforcement procedures for intellectual property rights, and the United States has refused to implement the changes in section 337 until the Uruguay Round negotiations on trade related aspects of intellectual property rights (TRIPs) are concluded. See Bureau of National Affairs, *International Trade Reporter*, November 15, 1989, pp. 1466–1468.
33. A common definition of dumping (governed by the GATT code of the Tokyo Round) is the sale of products for export at a price less than that for which those same products are sold at home. This definition turns out to be excruciatingly complex to apply. Dumping per se is not GATT-illegal, but GATT members can use antidumping duties to offset it, provided they can show that "material injury" (or threat thereof) is being caused.
34. Destler, *American Trade Politics*, p. 172. See also J. M. Finger, H. Keith Hall, and Douglas R. Nelson, "The Political Economy of Administered Protection," *American Economic Review* 72, no. 3 (June 1982), pp. 452–466.
35. Patrick A. Messerlin, "The Mexican Antidumping System: Two Years After" (Washington, D.C.: World Bank, 1988); and ———, *Antidumping Laws and Developing Countries*, World Bank Working Papers (Washington, D.C., 1988).
36. Gary N. Horlick, "The United States Antidumping System," in John H. Jackson and Edwin A. Vermulst, eds., *Antidumping Law and Practice: A Comparative Approach* (Ann Arbor, Mich.: University of Michigan Press, 1989), pp. 99–166. See also N. David Palmeter, "Review Essay: The Capture of the Antidumping Law," *Yale Journal of International Law* 14, no. 1 (Winter 1989), pp. 182–198.
37. EC data illustrate this phenomenon very clearly, showing a slow start after the first proceeding in 1970 and then a marked and rapid increase. Although other factors also contributed to this, the education campaign of European trade associations was instrumental in diffusing information on how to launch an antidumping proceeding. See Jean-Francois Bellis, "The EEC Antidumping System," in Jackson and Vermulst, *Antidumping*, pp.

42–44. See also Michael Davenport, *The Charybdis of E.C. Industrial Policy*, Royal Institute of International Affairs, paper no. 22 (London, 1989) and bibliography cited therein.
38. Finger, Hall, and Nelson, "The Political Economy of Administered Protection," p. 455.
39. *Inside U.S. Trade*, Washington, D.C.: Inside Washington Publication, September 15, 1989, p. 18.
40. ECAT, *1989 Issues Paper*, p. 16.
41. Bureau of National Affairs, *International Trade Reporter*, May 3, 1989, p. 553.
42. *Inside U.S. Trade*, September 22, 1989, p. 5.
43. *Inside U.S. Trade*, Special Report, November 17, 1989, pp. 51–56.
44. This summary is taken largely from International Division, U.S. Chamber of Commerce, *The Omnibus Trade and Competitiveness Act of 1988* (Washington, D.C., 1988), pp. 8–11.
45. Edwin A. Vermulst, "The Antidumping Systems of Australia, Canada, the EEC and the U.S.A.," in Jackson and Vermulst, *Antidumping*, p. 430.
46. Ibid., p. 431.
47. Brian Hindley, "Dumping and the Far East Trade of the European Community," *World Economy* (December 1988), p. 455.
48. Bellis, "EEC Antidumping," pp. 67–68.
49. Ibid., p. 45.
50. Edwin A. Vermulst, *Antidumping Law and Practice in the United States and the European Communities: A Comparative Analysis* (Amsterdam: North-Holland, 1987), pp. 497–498. See also Brian Hindley, "Unfair Trade and Unfair Trade Measures: Which Threatens the World Trading System?" (Paper presented at Commonwealth Seminar, London, July 18–20, 1988).
51. Hindley, "Dumping and the Far East Trade," pp. 446–447. The July 1988 codification represents a significant change in the provisions applicable to calculating margins from that previously followed. The change, which resulted in the "tilt" against products in electronics from Japan and the NIEs was developed by the Commission over the past few years. See Bellis, "EEC Antidumping," pp. 81–83.
52. William Lee and Robert Herzstein, "EC Dumping Law: A Growing Source of Trade Frictions," in *1992: The External Impact of European Unification, Part 2* (Washington, D.C.: Buraff Publications, Inc., July 28, 1989), p. 11.
53. "U.S. Chipmakers Accuse EC of Threatening Curbs," *The Washington Post*, August 2, 1989, p. F1.
54. Bureau of National Affairs, *International Trade Reporter*, March 29, 1989, p. 395.
55. William Dawkins, "Some original ideas on the limits to free trade," *Financial Times*, February 10, 1989, p. 9.
56. Ibid. A wise firm will hire a lawyer to get a binding origin status on a particular product. If, however, the origin status is "clarified" at a later date, the lawyer will have to go through an appeal system involving both national customs authorities and the European Court of Justice.
57. "Europe's trade policy: A gun that needs to get knotted," *Economist*, September 9, 1989, p. 82–85.
58. *Financial Times*, October 30, 1989, p. 4.

3. INNOVATION POLICY

1. See OECD, *Science and Technology Policy Outlook* (Paris, 1988), pp. 16–24. The term was first used in OECD, *Innovation Policy Trends and Perspectives* (Paris, 1982). A number of country reviews have been published, and more are under way.
2. See, for example, *Toronto Summit Economic Declaration*, June 21, 1988, p. 3; and OECD, *Economies in Transition: Structural Adjustment in OECD Countries* (Paris, 1989).
3. See, for example, William R. Cline, *American Trade Adjustment: The Global Impact* (Washington, D.C.: Institute for International Economics, 1989) and the bibliography therein.
4. Elizabeth Johnson and Donald Moggridge, eds., *The Collected Writings of John Maynard Keynes* (Cambridge, England: Cambridge University Press, 1983), vol. 7, p. 383.
5. For a useful review of the literature, see J. David Richardson, "Empirical Research on Trade Liberalisation with Imperfect Competition," *OECD Economic Studies*, no. 12 (1989); and Richard G. Harris, "The New Protectionism Revisited" (Innis Lecture, Canadian Economics Association Meetings, Quebec City, June 1989).
6. See bibliographies in Harris, "The New Protectionism Revisited," and Richardson, "Empirical Research on Trade Liberalisation." See also Bhagwati, "U.S. Trade Policy Today" and _____, "Is Free Trade Passe After All?," *Weltwirtschaftliches Archiv* (1989); and Anne O. Krueger, "Free Trade Is the Best Policy" (Paper presented at the Brookings Institution Conference on Alternative Trade Strategies for the United States, Washington, D.C., September 12, 1989).
7. Krueger, "Free Trade."
8. For an early example of the use of the term "strategic" in this sense, see Kenneth Flamm, *Targeting the Computer: Government Support and International Competition* (Washington, D.C.: Brookings Institution, 1987), pp. 174–175. The author describes the French response to U.S. export controls on shipments of high-performance computers, which led to a policy of protectionism and building "national champions."

    The notion of linkage externalities' stemming from intermediate goods and nontradeable inputs, which potentially extends the externalities argument, is described in Paul Krugman, "Strategic Sectors and International Competition," in Stern, *U.S. Trade Policy*, pp. 224–225.
9. Richardson, "Empirical Research," p. 15.
10. See, for example, Alan V. Deardorff and Robert M. Stern, "Current Issues in Trade Policy: An Overview," in Stern, *U.S. Trade Policy*, pp.15–68.
11. Henry Ergas, "Does Technology Policy Matter?" Centre for European Policy Studies, Paper no. 29 (Brussels, 1986).
12. See, for example, Herbert I. Fusfeld, *The Technical Enterprise: Present and Future Patterns* (New York: Ballinger, 1986); and Richard R. Nelson, *High-Technology Policies: A Five-Nation Comparison* (Washington, D.C.: American Enterprise Institute for Public Policy Research, 1984).

13. See, for example, Michael G. Borrus, *Competing for Control: America's Stake in Microelectronics* (New York: Ballinger, 1988); George C. Eads and Kozo Yamamura, "The Future of Industrial Policy," in Kozo Yamamura and Yasukichi Yasuba, *The Political Economy of Japan. Volume I: The Domestic Transformation* (Stanford, Calif.: Stanford University Press, 1987); Flamm, *Targeting the Computer;* Christopher Freeman, *Technology Policy and Economic Performance: Lessons from Japan* (Sussex: Science Policy Research Unit, University of Sussex, 1987); Chalmers Johnson, *MITI and the Japanese Miracle* (Stanford, Calif.: Stanford University Press, 1982); Stephen D. Krasner, "Trade Conflicts and the Common Defense: The United States and Japan," *Political Science Quarterly*, no. 5 (1986); Gary R. Saxonhouse, "What Is All This about 'Industrial Targeting' in Japan?," *World Economy* 6, no. 3 (September 1983), pp. 253–273; Kozo Yamamura, "Caveat Emptor: The Industrial Policy of Japan," in Paul R. Krugman, ed., *Strategic Trade Policy and the New International Economics* (Cambridge, Mass.: MIT Press, 1986); and John Zysman, *Governments, Markets and Growth: Financial Systems and the Politics of Industrial Change* (Ithaca, N.Y.: Cornell University Press, 1983).
14. See Robert F. Owen, "The Evolution in Japan's Relative Technological Competitiveness since the 1960's: A Cross-Sectional Time-Series Analysis," *Bank of Japan Monetary and Economic Studies* (Tokyo, 1988).
15. For a clear exposition of this view, see Bruce R. Scott, "National Strategies: Key to International Competition," in Bruce R. Scott and George C. Lodge, eds., *U.S. Competitiveness in the World Economy* (Boston: Harvard Business School Press, 1985). See also Paul Krugman, "The Narrow Moving Band, the Dutch Disease, and the Competitive Consequences of Mrs. Thatcher," *Journal of Development Economics* 27 (North-Holland, 1987), pp. 41–55.
16. Richard G. Lipsey and Wendy Dobson, eds., "Shaping Comparative Advantage," C.D. Howe Institute Policy Study, no. 2 (Toronto, 1984), pp. 133–134.
17. OECD, *Main Science and Technology Indicators* (Paris, 1989). U.S. public expenditure on R&D also dwarfs that of other countries. The figures in 1987 were U.S., $61.1 billion; Japan, $10 billion; Germany, $8 billion.
18. Fusfeld, *Technical Enterprise*, p. 123.
19. See OECD, *Science and Technology Policy Outlook*, pp. 31–48.
20. The NCRA removes the risk of per se illegal standards and provides a "rule of reason" standard. It also protects ventures from treble damage liability, but still leaves open the risk of antitrust suit. A number of proposals for further change are now being put forward. See Heritage Foundation, "High Definition Television: What the Federal Government Can Do," *Issue Bulletin*, no. 150 (August 1989).
21. Flamm, *Targeting the Computer*, p. 115.
22. Office of the Undersecretary of Defense for Acquisition, *Report of Defense Science Board Task Force on Defense Semiconductor Dependency* (Washington, D.C., February 1987). Cited in Flamm, *Targeting the Computer*, p. 117.
23. Thomas M. Jorde and David J. Teece, "Innovation, Cooperation and Antitrust," *High Technology Law Journal* 4, no. 1 (1989), pp. 3–4.
24. See, especially, Johnson, *MITI and the Japanese Miracle;* and Borrus, *Competing for Control*. For an opposing view, see Saxonhouse, "What Is All This."

25. Andrew Pollack, "America's Answer to Japan's MITI," *The New York Times*, March 5, 1989, p. F1.
26. David Mowery and Nathan Rosenberg, "New Developments in U.S. Technology Policy: Implications for Competitiveness and International Trade Policy," p. 13.
27. Ibid., p. 15. The NCMS excludes foreign firms from membership and restricts the transfer of technologies developed under its sponsorship to member-firms' foreign subsidiaries (p. 12).
28. See Arthur Denzau, *Trade Protection Comes to Silicon Valley* (St. Louis: Center for the Study of American Business, Washington University, 1988).
29. Flamm, *Targeting the Computer*, pp. 165–166. In 1984 Germany also established a major program largely as a consequence of the British and French initiatives. These moves also stimulated cooperative arrangements within the private sector.
30. Margaret Sharp, "European Technology: Does 1992 Matter?" (Sussex: Science Policy Research Unit, University of Sussex, 1989), p. 15. See also Wayne Sandholz and John Zysman, "1992: Recasting the European Bargain," *World Politics* XLII, no. 1 (October 1989).
31. Sharp, "European Technology," p. 18. See also Peter Ludlow, *Beyond 1992: Europe and Its Western Partners* (Brussels: Centre for European Policy Studies, 1989), p. 29.
32. Ludlow, *Beyond 1992*, p. 29.
33. JESSI Planning Group, *Jessi, Joint European Submicron Silicon* (Itzehoe, Germany, n.d.).
34. Bureau of International Affairs, *International Trade Reporter, Current Reports* 6 (1989), p 871.
35. JESSI Planning Group, *Jessi*.
36. European Information Technology Industry Roundtable, *White Paper on the European I.T. Industry and the Single Market* (Brussels, 1989), p. 13.
37. J. P. Morgan, *World Financial Markets*, November 10, 1989, p. 9.
38. Hale, "The Dollar Outlook," p. 12.
39. Bureau of International Affairs, *International Trade Reporter*, May 31, 1989, p. 684.
40. Bhagwati, "U.S. Trade Policy Today," pp. 45–46.

4. CONCLUSIONS

1. Christopher Freeman, *Technology Policy and Economic Performance: Lessons from Japan* (London: Pinter Press, 1987), pp. 55–90.
2. See Milton Friedman, "The Invisible Hand in Economics and Politics" (Inaugural Singapore Lecture, Institute of Southeast Asian Studies, Singapore, n.d.).
3. The green movement in Europe, which gained considerable strength in the June 1989 European parliamentary elections, has argued that less trade and more self-sufficiency in food is desirable for environmental policy reasons. Also, in many rich countries the issue of "food safety"—organic farming and so forth—has become important in the political arena. The danger of such perfectly legitimate social and political objectives' leading to blocking imports is fairly obvious. One way of approaching

this would be to establish a scientific panel at the GATT to determine the safety issue; then, if governments (in the name of consumer preference) wish to block food or agricultural imports that the panel judges scientifically safe, they should be required to compensate the exporting country. A surveillance mechanism as well as a fast-track dispute settlement system would be essential if this route were followed. Green protectionism, if it escalates, will have its most serious impact on exporters in the less-developed countries, who might well demand more than this compensation—perhaps an arrangement with the World Bank to convert to "environmentally oriented farming."

4. Herbert Giersch, "Europe 1992 in an Open World Order" (Hamburg, 1988). See also Albert Bressand, "Beyond Interdependence: 1992 as a Global Challenge" (Working paper for Council on Foreign Relations' study group on Europe, America and 1992, New York, February 28, 1989).

5. Possibly as a result of the pressure generated by the Structural Impediments Initiative, Japan's Fair Trade Commission announced in September 1989 the launch of a review of its law governing business practice. For an account of the key role of competition policy in the industrial policy of Japan, see Kozo Yamamura, "Caveat Emptor," pp. 174–200.

6. For a recent analysis, see Federal Reserve Bank of New York (FRBNY), "Explaining International Differences in the Cost of Capital," *Quarterly Review* (Summer 1989), pp. 7–28, and bibliography cited therein. See also John Zysman, *Governments, Markets and Growth*.

7. FRBNY, "Explaining International Differences," p. 20.

8. Ibid., p. 25.

9. This process has, in fact, started. The British government's approach has been to document the technical barriers to takeovers in European member-countries, which the Commission plans to deal with by legislation. Major differences in market culture will, however, remain. See *Financial Times*, November 27, 1989, p. 5.

10. See Laura Tyson, "Managed Trade: Making the Best of the 'Second' Best" (Paper prepared for the Brookings Institution Conference on Trade Policy, Washington, D.C., September 12, 1989). Tyson proposes "sectoral managed trade arrangements" for high-technology industries that would involve negotiation of rules for government and firm behavior. These could be either bilateral or multilateral. Her proposal touches on the same issue—policy convergence—but is sectoral and trade-oriented and includes "rules" for private companies' behavior as well. See also Bhagwati, *Protectionism*, for a different proposal: "an international consensus on the desirability of achieving a *broad* intrasectoral balance of artificial advantages in a *narrow* range of . . . industries" (p. 128).

11. See Hale, "The Dollar Outlook," p. 5. Preliminary data for 1989 suggest that equity capital inflows are now financing half the current account deficit, whereas they financed 15–20% in the early 1980s. See also Edward M. Graham and Paul R. Krugman, *Foreign Direct Investment in the United States* (Washington, D.C.: Institute for International Economics, 1989).

12. The failure of T. Boone Pickens to secure a seat on the Koito car parts manufacturer board was "the final straw that broke American patience," as the *Economist* put it ("Mergers and Acquisitions in Japan: Lifting a Barrier

or Two," August 12, 1989, p. 68), and stimulated the changes announced recently by the Ministry of Finance. On the United Kingdom's concern about "reciprocity," see "Reciprocity & the Art of the Deal," *Financial Times,* September 18, 1989, p. 42. There is a basic difference between Anglo-Saxon capital markets, on the one hand, and continental and Japanese markets, on the other.
13. Jagdish Bhagwati, "U.S. Trade Policy Today," p. 46.
14. For a presentation of such proposals, see Edwin A. Vermulst, "Antidumping Systems of Australia, Canada, the EEC and the U.S.A.," pp. 459–466; and Mark Koulen, "Some Problems of Interpretation and Implementation of the GATT Antidumping Code," ibid, pp. 366–373.
15. For a review and bibliography, see Phedon Nicolaides, *The Hydra of Safeguards: An Intractable Problem for the Uruguay Round?* (Discussion Paper no. 21, Royal Institute of International Affairs, London, 1989).
16. For a full exposition of this view, see Victoria Curzon Price and G. Curzon, "The GATT Non-Discrimination Principles (MFN and National Treatment) and the Rise of Material Reciprocity in International Trade" (Bruges: College of Europe, 1989).
17. See Bruce Stokes, "Multiple Allegiances," *National Journal,* November 11, 1989, p. 2756.
18. Ibid., pp. 2757–2758.

APPENDIX

*Council on Foreign Relations Study on
"The Search for Stability: Business and Government in
an Interdependent World"*

Kenneth W. Dam
Group Chairman
Sylvia Ostry
Group Director
C. Michael Aho
Director, International Trade Project
Alison M. von Klemperer
Assistant Director, International Trade Project
Dorothy Price
Rapporteur

INDIVIDUAL PARTICIPANTS

José Alvarez	Robert F. Dillon
Thomas Baba	Albert Dowden
Jagdish Bhagwati	George Eads
Michael Borrus	William D. Eberle
Lewis M. Branscomb	Bo Egerdal
Albert Bressand	Everett Ehrlich
J. Travis Brooks	Gerald Epstein
Ashton B. Carter	Henry Ergas
Hans Decker	Geza Feketekuty
George De Menil	Charles Ferguson
Sir Roy Denman	Hajime Furata
Rimmer De Vries	Richard N. Gardner
William Diebold, Jr.	Charles N. Goldman

David C. Gompert
Jamie Gough
Pehr G. Gyllenhammar
Shigeru Handa
Sidney Harman
Curtis A. Hessler
Michael Hinks-Edwards
Michael W. Hodin
Gary N. Horlick
Hiroo Inoue
Shafiqul Islam
Walter K. Joelson
Peter B. Kenen
Kiyoaki Kikuchi
Nobuyori Kodaira
Makuto Kuroda
Bruno Lamborghini
Rune Landin
Arlette Laurent
Warren Lavorel
Robert Lawrence
Charles Levy
Wingate Lloyd
James G. Lowenstein
Peter Ludlow
Manfredo Macioti
Amir Mahini
David Malone
Elizabeth Martella
Michael Mastanduno
Brian McDonald
Helen Milner
Mustafa Mohatarem
Rebecca Morales
Jeremiah Murphy
M. Ishaq Nadiri
Richard Nelson
Kazuo Nukazawa

Hirofumi Okuyama
Thomas Ostermueller
Thomas Patton
John E. Pearson
Peter G. Peterson
Corrado Pirzio-Biroli
Gordon T. Ray
Nicholas X. Rizopoulos
Renato Ruggiero
Richard J. Samuels
Michael A. Samuels
Gary R. Saxonhouse
Alexander Schaub
Michael P. Schulhof
Judith N. Shapiro
Daniel A. Sharp
Kunio Shimazu
Kojiro Shiojiri
Leonard S. Silk
Michael B. Smith
Edson W. Spencer
Linda Spencer
Joan E. Spero
Joseph T. Stewart
Alan Stoga
Bruce Stokes
Carmen Suro-Bredie
John Temple Swing
Toshio Takayama
Peter Tarnoff
Masao Uchibayashi
Paul W. Van Orden
Raymond Vernon
Enzo Viscusi
William N. Walker
David Walters
Richard S. Ward
Kenneth Wattman

Leonard Waverman
Frank A. Weil
Marina v.N. Whitman

Alan Wm. Wolff
Hideo Yamabe
John Zysman

CORPORATE PARTICIPANTS

Bristol-Myers
General Electric
General Motors
IBM
ITT
Kao
Matsushita
NEC
Pfizer

Philips Consumer Electronics
Siemens
Sony
Squibb
Takeda Chemical Industries
Toyota
TRW
Unisys
Volvo

GLOSSARY OF ABBREVIATIONS AND ACRONYMS

ACTN	Advisory Committee for Trade Negotiations
ACTPN	Advisory Committee on Trade Policy and Negotiations (new name of ACTN, 1988)
BRITE	Basic Research in Industrial Technologies for Europe
CCC	Customs Cooperation Council
CEFIC	European Chemical Industry
CEO	Chief executive officer
CVD	Countervailing duty
DARPA	Defense Advanced Research Projects Agency (United States)
DRAM	Dynamic random access memory
EC	European Community
ECAT	Emergency Committee for American Trade
EEC	European Economic Community
ESPRIT	European Strategic Programme for Research in Information Technology
FRBNY	Federal Reserve Bank of New York
FTA	Free trade agreement
G-7	Group of Seven (United States, Japan, Germany, France, United Kingdom, Italy, and Canada)
GATS	General Agreement on Trade in Services
GATT	General Agreement on Tariffs and Trade
IC	Integrated circuits
IMF	International Monetary Fund
IPC	Intellectual Property Rights Committee
IT	Information technology
JESSI	Joint European Semiconductor Silicon Project
JETRO	Japan External Trade Organization
MCC	Microelectronics and Computer Technology Corporation

MFN	Most favored nation
MITI	Ministry of International Trade and Industry, Japan
MTN	Multilateral trade negotiations
NCMS	National Center for Manufacturing Sciences
NCRA	National Cooperative Research Act
NIE	Newly industrializing economies
OECD	Organization for Economic Cooperation and Development
R&D	Research and development
RACE	Research in Advanced Communication Systems for Europe
SIA	Semiconductor Industry Association
SII	Structural Impediments Initiative
TRIP	Trade Related Aspects of Intellectual Property Rights
UN	United Nations
UNICE	Union of Industries of the European Community
USTR	United States trade representative
VER	Voluntary export restraint
VLSI	Very large scale integrated circuit
WIPO	World Intellectual Property Organization

INDEX

Administrative Reform Council, 37
Advisory Committee on Trade Policy and Negotiations (ACTPN), 19–20, 21, 23, 25, 27, 29
Aggressive reciprocity policy, 29
Agriculture, 32, 36, 76–77
Alvey program, 71
Antidumping Act of 1921, 42
Antidumping laws, 40–42; competition policy as replacement for, 11, 91; dumping, definition of, 41, 103n33; GATT policy on, 90–96; rules of origin, 48–51; safeguard arrangement to deal with "fair" trade, 93–94; strategic industries and, 91. *See also* EC antidumping laws; U.S. antidumping laws
Antitrust law, U.S., 66, 67–68
Asia-Pacific Economic Co-Operation initiative, 14

Ball bearings antidumping case, 43–44
Bank for International Settlements, 7, 88
Banks, role in investment performance, 85–86
Basic Research in Industrial Technologies for Europe (BRITE), 73
Baucus, Max, 30
Bell Laboratories, 67
Brazil, 12
Bretton Woods system, 26
Brock, William, 27
Business Roundtable, 19
Byrd, Robert, 30

Canada, 12–13, 63
Chamber of Commerce, 19

Chemical industry, 32
Commerce, U.S. Department of, 42
Competition policy, 11, 84–85, 91
Congress, U.S., 20, 98
Connally, John, 26
Consortia, government-financed, 87–88
Convergence of domestic micro policy areas, 81–83; GATT policy proposals, 90–96; global corporations and, 96–99; OECD policy proposals, 83–90
Counterfeiting code, proposed, 3
"Created" comparative advantage, 55
Customs Cooperation Council (CCC), 50

Davignon, Viscomte, 71
Defense, U.S. Deparment of, 67, 68
Defense Advanced Research Projects Agency (DARPA), 68
Dekker, Wisse, 72
Denmark, 61
Dollar crisis, 7
Dollar depreciation, 10
Dumping, definition of, 41, 103n33

Eastman Kodak Company, 29–30
Economist, 51
Emergency Committee for American Trade (ECAT), 19, 29, 43
Environmental movement, 80, 107n3
European Chemical Industry (CEFIC), 32
European Commission: antidumping laws and, 46, 47, 49, 51; high trade policymaking, 30–35, 39
European Community (EC): account imbalances, 10; competition

policy, 11; Council of Ministers, 47; regional trading (*See* Europe 1992 program); semiconductor agreement with Japan, 51; "unfairness" in trade, policy toward, 45; U.S., trade relationship with, 10–11

EC antidumping laws: administration of, 46–47; circumvention issue, 48–49; dumping margins, calculation of, 47–48, 104n51; opposition within Community, 51–52; rules of origin, 48–50

EC high trade policy: bureaucratic policymaking system, 31–32; "closed" policymaking process, 30–31; GATT and Europe 1992 policymaking, differences between, 33–35; inertial tendency, 33; internal policy pressures, 31; private-sector input, 23, 32, 33–35; Triad high policy political economy, asymmetry in, 38–39

EC innovation policy: future prospects, 74–75; information technology field, 70–73; targeting of particular sectors and technologies, 73–74; technology diffusion focus, 61

European Court of Justice, 46

European Information Technology Industry Roundtable, 71, 74

European Roundtable, 33, 34–35, 72

European Strategic Programme for Research in Information Technology (ESPRIT), 71–72

European Technology Community, 70

Europe 1992 program, 12, 13; convergence of policy areas, 81–82; political economy of policymaking, 33–34

Filière Electronique R&D program, 71

Financial Times, 50

First-mover advantage, 60

Flexible manufacturing, 15

Foreign direct investment flows: differences within Triad, 87; by Japan, 76

France, 37, 65, 71

General Agreement on Tariffs and Trade (GATT), 1; agriculture issue, 76–77; antidumping issue, 90–96; bilateralist tendencies and, 12–13, 14; continuing negotiations, need for, 94–96; counterfeiting code, proposed, 3; EC policy toward (*See* EC high trade policy); innovation policy and, 6, 89; intellectual property issue, 23–24; investment and, 76; Japanese policy toward (*See* Japanese high trade policy); market access negotiations, 95; problems of, 1, 3; R&D subsidy issue, 87; safeguard arrangement to deal with "fair" trade, 93–94; stability as purpose of, 3; tariffs, focus on, 80; Tokyo Round, 20–21, 80; Uruguay Round, issues addressed at, 5; U.S. policy toward (*See* U.S. high trade policy)

Germany, West, 61; account surplus, 10; banks and corporations, relations between, 85–86; private-sector R&D expenditures, 65

Global corporations, 1–2; convergence of domestic micro policy areas, role in, 96–99; GATT-based system of rules, failure to develop, 3–4; governments, interactions with, 2; investment decisions, 15–16; neutrality strategy, 97–98; rules-based multilateral system, interest in preserving, 2–3; truly "global" multinationals, absence of, 82; U.S. high trade policy and, 25–26

Government role in economy, changing ideas about, 57–60

Green protectionism, 80, 107n3

Group of Seven (G-7), 53; account imbalances, 7; macro policy positions, incompatibility of, 6; multilateral surveillance of macro policy, 88–89, 90
Gyllenhammar, Pehr, 33

High-definition television, 68
High trade policy. *See* EC high trade policy; Japanese high trade policy; U.S. high trade policy

IBM, 44, 67
India, 12
Information and communication technology: EC innovation policy and, 70–73; as new techno-economic paradigm, 79–80
Innovation policy, 11–12; background conditions for initiation of, 53–57; blurring of boundaries between domestic and international policy, 75–78; comparative analysis of policy set, need for, 84–88; convergence of policy areas and, 82; definition of, 6, 53; economic theory and, 57–61; externalities rationale, 58, 59–60; GATT and, 6, 89; global current account imbalances and, 55; government-corporate interface component, 53; government role in economy, ideas about, 57–60; OECD policy proposals, 83–90; policy ambience for, 54–55; policy spillover within Triad, 75; R&D-related concerns ("first-mover" rationale), 60; rent-shifting rationale, 58–59; strategic industries and, 60, 84; structural adjustment initiative and, 53–55; technology development model, 61; technology diffusion model, 61; world trade growth and, 55, 56. *See also* EC innovation policy; Japanese innovation policy; U.S. innovation policy
Intel company, 49

Intellectual property issue: counterfeiting code, proposed, 3; European corporations and, 35; GATT and, 23–24
Intellectual Property Rights Committee (IPC), 23–24
International Monetary Fund (IMF), 1, 4, 89
International Trade Commission, 42
Investment: corporate investment decisions, 15–16; foreign direct investment flows, 76, 87; as GATT issue, 76; technology flows and, 1–2
Investment performance, analysis of, 85–86

Japan: account adjustment process, 9; banks and corporations, relations between, 85–86; Fifth Generation Program, 70–71, 72; foreign direct investment, 76, 87, 109n12; high-technology sectors, success in, 55, 56; import propensity, 9–10; interventionist policy mix of 1950s and 1960s, 62–64; market structure (*keiretsu*), 67, 86; regional trading, 13–14; semiconductor agreement with EC, 51. *See also* U.S.–Japanese trade relationship
Japanese high trade policy: bureaucratic governance, system of, 35–36; "closed" policymaking process, 30–31; MITI-business interface, 37–38; political input, 35; private sector, role of, 23, 36–37; Triad high policy political economy, asymmetry in, 38–39
Japanese innovation policy: information and communication technology, exploitation of, 80; market structure and, 67; private-sector R&D expenditures, 65; reverse engineering and, 63; targeting particular sectors and technologies, 62–64; technology development and diffusion, 61–62

Japan External Trade Organization (JETRO), 36
Joint European Semiconductor Silicon project (JESSI), 73–74

Keidanren (Japanese business coalition), 23, 24, 36–37
Keynes, J. M., 3, 19, 57
Korea, South, 51
Kyoto Convention, 50

Level playing field concept, 90
Low-track policy. *See* Antidumping laws; Trade remedy laws

Mansfield, Mike, 30
Microelectronics and Computer Technology Corporation (MCC), 66
Micron company, 44
Ministry of International Trade and Industry, Japanese (MITI), 36, 62, 63, 66, 72; business community and, 37–38
Multi Fibre Arrangement, 94
Multilateral surveillance of macro policy, 88–89, 90

National Association of Manufacturers, 19
National Center for Manufacturing Sciences (NCMS), 68
National Cooperative Research Act (NCRA) of 1984, 66, 106n20
New international trade theory, 57–58
Newly industrializing economies (NIEs), 9, 55
New York Times, 68
Nixon, Richard M., 26
Noyce, Robert, 73–74

OECD *Outlook*, 7
Omnibus Trade and Competitiveness Act of 1988, 7, 9, 21, 29, 43
113 Committee, 31
Organization for Economic Cooperation and Development (OECD), 53; Business and Industry Advisory Committee, 4; innovation policy proposals, 83–90

Pacific area trading bloc, 13–14
Plaza Accord of 1985, 28
Pluralist activism, 18–20, 38–39
Political economy of trade policymaking, 2, 17–18; conventional model of, 18; Triad high policy political economy, asymmetry in, 38–39. *See also* EC high trade policy; Japanese high trade policy; U.S. high trade policy
Protectionism: Green protectionism, 80, 107n3; "new" protectionism, 4–5; product-specific protection, 18–19; in R&D policy, 60, 87–88. *See also* Antidumping laws
Pro Trade Group, 43

R&D: expenditures by private sector, 15, 65–66; protectionism and, 60, 87–88
Reagan, Ronald, 28
Regional trading blocs, 12–14
Research in Advanced Communication Systems for Europe (RACE), 73
Reverse engineering, 63
Ricoh company, 49
Ronald Thatcher revolution, 54
Rules of origin, 48–51

Section 301 unfair trade investigations, 28–29, 30, 44–45
Sectoral managed trade arrangements, 108n10
Security and trade, linking of, 26
Sematech venture, 66–67, 68
Semiconductor Industry Association (SIA), 44, 69
Semiconductors: EC-Japanese agreement on, 51; U.S.–Japanese dispute regarding, 38, 44, 69–70; U.S. policy to promote production, 66–67

INDEX □ 121

Smart, S. Bruce, 38
Smith, Adam, 57
Strategic industries, 11; antidumping laws and, 91; definition of, 60, 84
Strauss, Robert, 21
Structural adjustment initiative, 53–55, 81
Structural Impediments Initiative (SII), 77–78, 81, 86
Subsidy–countervailing duty (CVD) cases, 40–41
Superconductivity Competitiveness Initiative, 68
Sweden, 61

Targeting of particular sectors and technologies, 11; in EC, 73–74; in Japan, 62–64
Television industry, 51
Texas Instruments, 44
Time magazine, 81
Trade Act of 1974, 20, 28
Trade Agreements Program, 28
Trade Reform Action Coalition, 44
Trade remedy laws, 39–42; changes over time, 42; complexity of, 40. *See also* Antidumping laws

Uncertainty in world trading system: costs of, 4; macro background factors, 6–11; micro background factors, 11–12; reduction of uncertainty, importance of, 98–99; regional trading blocs and, 12–14
"Unfairness" in trade: categories of unfair practices, 45; EC policy toward, 45; GATT safeguard arrangement regarding, 93–94; U.S. policy toward, 26–30, 44–46; unequal access issue, 9
Union of Industries of the European Community (UNICE), 23, 24
United Kingdom, 65, 71
United States: antitrust laws, 66, 67–68; competitiveness problems, 8, 10, 11–12; EC, trade relationship with, 10–11; foreign direct investment, 87; regional trading, 12–13
U.S. account imbalances: "crisis" rhetoric regarding, 8; dollar depreciation and, 10; domestic reactions to, 8; international reactions to, 7; Japanese trading practices and, 9–10; micro policies in response to, 8–10, 55
U.S. antidumping laws: administration of, 42–43; anti-antidumping pressure, 43–44; circumvention issue, 43; history of, 42; unfair practices targeted by, 44–46
U.S.–Canada Free Trade Agreement (FTA), 12–13
U.S. high trade policy: ambivalence toward multilateralism (mid-1980s), 27–28; antidumping laws and, 44–46; conventional model of, 18; counterweight system of trade politics, 20; exploitation of split among economists regarding policy prescriptions, 30; global corporations and, 25–26; government system, reflection of, 18; intellectual property issue, 23–24; market-opening approach, 26–30; multitrack policy without defined objectives, 25, 28–30; private-sector advisory system, 20–25; private-sector role (pluralist activism), 18–20, 38–39; Triad high policy political economy, asymmetry in, 38–39
U.S. innovation policy: cooperative research projects, 66–67; corporate organization and strategy, 66; fragmentation and diversity in, 65; government policy, changes in, 66–67; market structure issue, 67–68; military spending and, 68; private-sector R&D expenditures, 65–66; semiconductor arrangement with

Japan, 69–70; technology development focus, 61
U.S.–Japanese Semiconductor Agreement of 1986, 29, 44, 51, 69–70
U.S.–Japanese trade relationship: Japanese account adjustment process, 9; "Japanese-are-so-different-that-special-rules-are-required-only-for-them" view, 82–83; semiconductor dispute, 38, 44, 69–70; Structural Impediments Initiative (SII), 77–78, 81, 86; U.S. frustration regarding imbalances, 9; U.S. market-opening policy, 26–27, 29–30
U.S. Memories (joint venture), 67
U.S. trade representative (USTR), 21

Very Large Scale Integrated Circuit (VLSI) Program, 72

World Bank, 1, 4
World Intellectual Property Organization (WIPO), 23–24

Yeutter, Clayton, 23

ABOUT THE AUTHOR

Sylvia Ostry is chairman and senior research fellow at the Centre for International Studies, University of Toronto, and chairman of The National Council of the Canadian Institute for International Affairs. She was the 1988–89 Volvo distinguished visiting fellow at the Council on Foreign Relations in New York.

After teaching and research at various Canadian universities and at the University of Oxford Institute of Statistics, Dr. Ostry joined the federal government in 1964. Among the posts she held were: ambassador for multilateral trade negotiations and prime minister's personal representative for the economic summit (1985–88); and deputy minister for international trade and coordinator of international economic relations (1984–85). She also served as head of the economics and statistics department of the OECD (1979–83), and as chairman of the Economic Council of Canada (1978–79).

Dr. Ostry is an Officer of the Order of Canada, the recipient of the Oustanding Achievement Award from the government of Canada, and of 17 honorary degrees from universities in Canada and abroad. Among the many articles and books of which she is author or co-author are: with Michael Artis, *International Economic Policy Coordination* (1986); *Interdependence: Vulnerability and Opportunity* (1987); and with C. Michael Aho, "Regional Trading Blocs: Pragmatic or Problematic?," in Brock and Hormats, *The Global Economy: America's Role in the Decade Ahead* (1989).

The Council on Foreign Relations publishes authoritative and timely books on international affairs and American foreign policy. Designed for the interested citizen and specialist alike, the Council's rich assortment of studies covers topics ranging from economics to regional conflict to U.S.–Soviet relations. If you would like more information, please write:

Council on Foreign Relations Press
58 East 68th Street
New York, NY 10021
Telephone: (212) 734-0400
FAX: (212) 861-1789

GOVERNMENTS & CORPORATIONS IN A SHRINKING WORLD

"Interesting and provocative—a classic example of Sylvia Ostry's rare ability to look 'over the horizon' and identify both looming hazards and needed precautions."
 William E. Brock III, former Secretary of Labor (1985–1987) and U.S. Trade Representative (1981–1983)

"Ostry has written a thoughtful, in-depth analysis of the complex problems that have emerged in the globalization of corporations. This book should be read by anyone involved in international trade."
 Michael P. Schulhof, Director, Sony Corporation, and Vice Chairman, Sony Corporation of America

"Ostry explores the dynamic, exciting developments in public policy where business and government work together to build a more productive, wealth-creating world economy. She applies intelligence and broad governmental experience to a fascinating subject for all those interested in international trade and investment policy."
 Edmund T. Pratt, Jr., Chairman and CEO, Pfizer, Inc.

Global stability has been placed at risk by economic conflict within the Triad: the U.S., Europe, and Japan. Ostry argues that the health of the world economy will be determined by the interaction of global corporations and national governments in the Triad, not by governments and international organizations alone. She presents the first examination of the interrelationship between corporate behavior and government policy evolution. In a systematic analysis of trade and innovation policies in the Triad that focuses on the most radically divergent and often discordant policies, Ostry recommends new and urgently needed initiatives to prevent dangerous economic confrontation and to optimize competition.

THE AUTHOR

Sylvia Ostry is Chairman and Senior Research Fellow at the Centre for International Studies, University of Toronto, and Chairman of The National Council of the Canadian Institute for International Affairs. From 1985–1988, she was the Canadian Ambassador for Multilateral Trade Negotiations and the Prime Minister's Personal Representative for the Economic Summit.

Cover Design: Whit Vye

0-87609-079-X

$14.95

LIBRARY OF DAV   GE